CONVERSATIONS ON PASTORAL SURVIVAL

MICHAEL HURDMAN

dustjacket

www.dustjacket.com

Table of Contents

Foreword

In one of the greatest chapters of the New Testament, we find these words written by the apostle Paul, " for now we see through a glass darky, but then face to face; now I know in part; but then shall I know even as also I am known" (I Corinthians 13:12).

The call to lead and serve God's people as a pastor and leader is a calling to fulfill a relationship of trust from God to feed his flock, and, love each member of the flock as the Good Shepherd loves us. However, the journey or path on which this under shepherd walks is of a mixed terrain. At times, the terrain is ladened with rich soil due to fresh rains; in some places, the terrain is flat and even; while at other places, the terrain is unstable which allows for debris to flow in, tension cracks develop, and gullies are formed. Yet, it is often in those moments of instability, that the pastor/leader is overwhelmed and tempted to question that which God has called him or her to. However, this questioning or reexamine of one's call through a fresh introspection of grace is a reminder that the glass through which we look is distorted by our own human frailties and weaknesses, yet, God sees us as we are and uses us anyway.

In this book, Rev. Michael Hurdman, honestly, yet, poignantly, insists that if we are to lead and minister to the best of our understanding and ability, we have to be willing to look within by asking our self some hard questions. Michael Jackson, the renowned Pop singer sang it this way, "I'm looking at the man in the mirror; I'm asking him to change his ways", therefore, if we, as pastors and leaders, really want to experience success in the calling God has given to us and effectively serve those we shepherd, we have to do our part to change our ways. How do we do this? Rev. Hurdman moves us to first look "inward" in order to be our best "outward", for the "outward" should always point us to how we can best serve others. The inward look is not comfortable and will pull at the core of the soul, but if we go through the process, we'll certainly be better because of it.

The conversational style that Rev. Hurdman uses in this writing reflects his relationship as a fellow journeyman, not an authority on the topic; yet, he writes from lessons learned through his own successes and failures, and he passes them on with honesty and in hope that the reader will gain courage and receive correction to 'change his ways' in order to not simply survive, but to thrive.

Kimberly S. Carter Thomas, D.Min.
Professor, Christian Ministries
Mid America Christian University

Acknowledgements

Nothing of any significance happens in isolation. This book is not the product of one person, anymore than a life is the product of the individual. We are the product of what many people have poured into us. While the road to get here as been difficult at times, I realize this book is a byproduct of all of the good and bad experiences. If God had not allowed me to experience the life I have, there would be no book. Therefore, all thanks and glory be given to God. That being said, there are so many people that have been a part of my growth that need to be mentioned. That, in itself, seems so little, when so much more should be said. I am so thankful to my wife. All of those nights she stayed up typing papers, taking care of the children and working a full-time job while I was in college. All of those years when she did without, supported me and worked along side of me as a pastor's wife. Then, when I wanted to go back to school she was there again, giving me the time to do the work. Thanks to my two daughters, Laura and Pamela for loving me, even though I didn't give you the time you needed and deserved. Thank you for becoming godly women, raising godly children of your own, and doing a better job than I did. I am especially thankful to Dr. Kimberly Thomas for having the confidence in me. She not only hired me as an adjunct, but also as a full-time faculty member. She has allowed me to be creative and to see what God has done in my life. There have been times that she has challenged me to be and do more. Her encouragement concerning this book and its use in classes and conferences has meant a great deal to me. Two years ago, when I first thought about actually writing the book, I asked Dr. Chuck Crow if he would like to write it with me. He said he really did not want to commit the time, but I should do it. It was during many of those "conversations" that much of the material in this book was birthed. He gave much needed insight and advice. I also want to express my appreciation to Reverend Steve Chiles. Steve is a brother and my pastor, who mentors many pastors and is a gifted speaker and leader. He consented to make some recommendations regarding content, which I have incorporated. Special thanks has to go to Deniece Chaplin, for the many readings and editing for spelling, punctuation and wording. She made many great recommendations for changing the way I said things. Her words of encouragement and the value she placed on the book were even more appreciated than the editing. Finally, I want to thank Adam Toler, the publisher of "Conversations on Pastoral Survival," for the design and publication. He made the process easy and created an attractive work.

Introduction

I have often wondered why authors have a preface to their books. Why didn't they just get to the subject matter? Was the preface just something to give the book the needed number of pages? This book could use more pages. I also realized that when I saw "Preface" I would turn the page to get to the book. However, I would read the introduction to a book. Consequently, I decided to have an introduction instead of a preface. I will preface by saying that this book does not try to give all the answers. The goal of what follows is to make you aware of the issues and to encourage you to work on the solutions. I do not think there are any quick fixes. What I point out, concerning some of the problems inherent in ministry, will not be fixed with one little adjustment. You cannot Google, "How to fix my ministry and make it more satisfying." It is a lot like golf. It doesn't take a professional but a few moments to point out the problems with your golf game. The problem lies in the fact that it is not just one thing, and in trying to concentrate on one thing another aspect of your game is still bad and your score doesn't improve. Your game only improves when you can do things naturally. If you have to think about too many things at the same time nothing goes right. To have a good golf game takes commitment to practice doing the right things. So, when it comes to the issues in this book, it will take a commitment to working at the solutions. At the end of most chapters I will provide a bibliography that will be books and articles I used to write about the material in the chapter. I will also make some recommendations for further reading. I will be providing the survival tips, but you will need to go to the necessary material referenced to be better informed.

The pages of this book are a product of a conference I did for the state of Alabama Church of God ministers. The material is very conversational in style because it is about issues in which I have had many conversations. It is also material I have taught to aspiring ministers at Mid-America Christian University. The title, "Conversations on Pastoral Survival," really is what I believe can make the difference in surviving or dying pastorally. I have focused on what I believe to be real issues for many serving in ministry, realizing that these are not the only issues. As I have shared my concerns, I have had others disagree with me and instead say, the problems are in other areas. I am sure there are more problems in regards to ministry than I have dealt with in the pages of this book. However, these are issues that are generally faced by many pastors in churches of 125 members or less. I almost think it is similar to how John ends his gospel concerning all that Jesus did. He said it was not possible to mention all he [Jesus] did and that it would take many books to cover his ministry. There are in fact, many books written on each of the chapters contained herein. I am not saying anything original, and if it had not been for people who have written extensively on the material in this book, there would be no book. Many have given extensive treatment on the issues and some very helpful solutions. This is an attempt to consolidate and condense some of the material I have read and to prod you to work on the solutions.

They say, "Hind sight is 20/20," but it is not nearly as helpful as foresight. I hope this gives some foresight. As I have reflected back on ministry, some things became very obvious to me concerning things I did not know while I was a pastor. I can testify to the difference that facing some of the issues and working on the solutions highlighted herein has made in me and in my current ministry. I suppose I should do a disclaimer and say, "My results may not be the same for everyone." And while I am no longer serving as a pastor, it is with great anticipation that this will make a difference in you and your ministry.

I am sure that you are doing everything you know to do, but if you are like I was, you are finding that it isn't enough. We can institute programs, develop mission statements, do strategic planning, and still nothing changes. Perhaps you have even questioned if you have missed your calling and are beginning to consider leaving the ministry. Don't give up hope of a fulfilling ministry. No, this book will not fix everything, but I sincerely believe it will give some direction that can lead you to becoming more effective.

I know that what I have discovered and begun to work on has made a significant difference in the way I minister and in the response I have received from ministry. I did not write this to make money or make a name for myself. I wrote this wanting to help you.

Before you begin reading, there is one more thing I want to say. While I truly believe this will be helpful to your ministry, it will take some intentionality on your part to be of any value. However, even with concentrated effort, that will not be enough. You will need the Holy Spirit to work on areas of need. It will be a daily, and even a moment-by-moment work, for which you will need his help. Be that as it may, I believe that is what God wants anyhow; dependence on him.

SURVIVAL TIP #1

Realize You Don't Even Know
What You Don't Know

W hy is this book necessary? I recently learned that I am creative and a nurturer by nature. Therefore, it seems quite natural to want to create something that would be helpful. Years of experience tells me I have something to share that others could benefit from. This first chapter comes from those years of experience. My experience may not be the same as yours, but maybe there is something of value that will resonate with you. Hopefully, there will be those times as you read, when you find yourself thinking, "I know exactly what you mean

It occurred to me that there is in some regard a resemblance between the NFL and the pastoral ministry. That resemblance is not in salary comparison, type of talent needed, or the fan base. The NFL has recently been addressing the issue of concussions in players. The problem

1

is greater than just the initial results of the devastating hit incurred on a football field. The effects are manifested years down the road in psychological and physical ramifications that are life threatening. You have seen it happen; a receiver is running across the field, just about to catch a pass and out of nowhere a defensive back hits him from the blind side. He lays motionless on the field for a moment, and the trainer runs on to the field. When they finally get the receiver up, he looks around and asks if anyone got the license number of that truck that hit him. He wonders, "What happened?" That happens in ministry too. We do not get tackled by a 250 pound linebacker, but we can be left asking, "What happened?" Part of this book is to look at what happens that causes men and women, committed to ministry, to leave that ministry, and wonder "what happened?" Of course, there are always going to be those who will judgmentally ask the same question.

The question, "What happened," began in graduate school. I had to write a thesis before they would let me graduate. It had to be something that was applicable to ministry. Having just left being a pastor, with no intention of returning to that life, I wanted to know what were the contributing factors that had brought me to this place. While my study began by looking at material related to why minister's leave the ministry, it eventually brought me to how to be more effective in ministry. I managed to write that thesis and surprisingly, they allowed me to graduate. That thesis was enough to satisfy graduation requirements, but it wasn't very helpful. It sat in my book case for several years as a testimony of my successfully finishing school. My last year of graduate school I was given the opportunity to do adjunct work for Mid-America Christian University. Dr. Kimberly Tomas asked me if I would like to teach a class in homiletics as an adjunct instructor. That would lead to teaching on a regular basis Bible and ministry classes to undergraduate students in the Adult School of Ministry. Then, in 2015 I was given the privilege to become a full time faculty member at Mid America Christian University. I work with some truly brilliant people. There have been some great discussions about ministry that once again stirred that desire in me to help pastors. It is out of those discussions that I had the privilege to share much of what I have learned with other pastors, and had what I shared validated. This became the impetus to write this book. I sit across from a psychiatrist everyday who teaches in the Master's program. I get a lot of free counseling. I asked him about my study into why ministers leave the ministry, and asked him if he thought the study was an effort to try and come to some kind of healing for myself? He said, "It certainly could be," and after reflection I can assure you it certainly has been for me. I hope it will do the same for you.

I do not think my circumstances were a great deal different from what many will experience, or are presently experiencing. As I recall the process I went through, perhaps you will relate to it as well. What happened? I had sensed the call of God on my life and the church confirmed it in my life. I wanted to preach the Gospel. I couldn't understand why I couldn't just take my Bible and start preaching. The church said, "You need some training. You need to go to Bible College." I agreed and started the process, and enrolled in Bible College. My wife, Barbara, and I prayed and believed that going to Bible college was what God would have us to do. We were both scared and excited at the same time, realizing this was a big step of faith. We also believed we were on our way to a wonderful adventure. We were going to be used by God, and would be making an impact on people's lives for eternity. I was 31, my wife was 30 and we both had good, secure jobs that we left behind. We packed up the UHaul truck and, with our two daughters drove across the country to go to school. We were a typical Bible College family. We both worked and I went to school. Back then, computers were things at NASA, not something you could carry around with you. My wife stayed up late typing all of my papers on a portable manual typewriter. Correcting papers meant using those messy bottles of white paint. I took all the required courses, and even took extra courses. I worked a full-time job and went to school for three years. I spent hours writing papers and sitting in class under men and women who had served decades in ministry. If anyone knew about ministry, surely these men and women were qualified to teach me. I learned about Bible history, church polity, how to prepare a sermon, conduct a funeral and enough Greek to make me dangerous. Did I tell you I learned Bible, history, church polity and how to prepare a sermon? I am sure there were other useful classes believed to be necessary for effective ministry that I endured. That is probably an accurate assessment of what I did; I endured them. I am certain I was taught everything the Church thought I would need to get a good start. Graduation came, and I walked across the stage and received my diploma. Of the 600 students that started when I did 60% had dropped out. Unfortunately, in 1979 the attitude of the Church was, "If you are really called of God you will make it." I wish I could say that those years prepared me for what was ahead. Still today, as we graduate students, there is no way to give them everything they need. I tell my students, "You don't even know what you don't know."

I went to my first church excited and scared. It was a mission church with about 13 people. I knew nothing about church planting. I didn't care. I didn't expect to start big, but believed between God and me, we would grow this little flock. I worked hard, studied and prepared sermons. I knocked on doors, had revivals, fasted and prayed. Our first building was a dance studio. There were mirrors on one wall for the dancer's to see themselves. When we had church services, I was tempted to count the people in the mirror, as well as the few that sat in the congregation. There were some high water marks when we had as many as 50. There were more times when it was just the 13, and sometimes when it was just my wife and children. Seven years later, and an economic downturn saw my entire congregation move.

Undeterred, I accepted a call to another church, which required me to serve as school principal as well as pastor.

I had never been a school principal. My only experience with a school principal was in seventh grade when I was sent to his office for misbehavior. A year after coming to the church, the congregation decided to relocate and build. This was great to me because it fit my skills. I had been a carpenter for many years and had helped build a new facility where I became a Christian. So, this was an added benefit for the church. Now, I was pastor, principal, and contractor. I worked hard, studied and prepared sermons, fasted, prayed, and wept. Four years later I felt it was time to move on and I accepted a call to another church. For the next 14 years, I worked hard, studied and prepared sermons. I tried everything that came down the pike in church growth. We had revivals, and did I say, I fasted, prayed, and wept? If you are thinking, "Yeah, but did you....?" I'm sure I did that too. I can say that in 26 years I literally gave blood, sweat and tears to pastoral ministry just like what you have done, and are probably still doing. For most of my ministry, I worked a secular job along with my pastoral duties. This is the life of most pastors today. They are pastors who work as carpenters, bus drivers, school teachers, or a hundred other noble vocations. They do this so they can have the privilege to preach on Sundays and Wednesday nights. With pastoring a small church comes the added benefit of humility and a small paycheck. We sacrificed and did without, just as most pastors and their families do in small churches. You and I would say, "It's worth it". Unfortunately, the only thing my family did without wasn't having the things that others had. Too often, they did without having a husband

and a father, because I was too busy being a pastor. I was too busy meeting everyone else's needs and expectations and I neglected the people most important; my family.

There were some great moments when I was preaching. The Holy Spirit would be so powerfully present. There were other times when I would have liked the floor to open up and swallow me like the earth, just as it did with Achan in the Old Testament. I saw lives transformed by the power of God, and I watched as people drifted away, and their lives were ruined. I did plenty of baby dedications and baptisms. I also did many funerals, and wept with families as they said their final words to loved ones. There were Sunday mornings I could hardly wait to get in the pulpit, but there were way too many Mondays when I wanted to resign. There were too many weeks, months and years when the church just did not appear to be progressing. When I say progressing read, "growing" there. The people were loving, and many became good friends. We went on trips together and laughed so hard we cried. We worked side by side changing oil in widows and single mom's cars, and handing out groceries to people in need. I would come up with another wild and crazy ministry, and people would get excited and follow my leadership. I can certainly say, "I was loved."

I know what you must be thinking. How could anyone walk away from that? Part of it had to do with all those Monday mornings I resigned, and the Saturday nights when I believed Sunday was going to be different. After 14 years, the church had some different faces, but it was about the same size. I considered taking another church, but just couldn't see starting again, thinking that it would be different. The little engine that could, no longer could. My children had grown, gone to college, married and left home. My oldest daughter, Laura, called me from Oklahoma City and told me that the Christian school she worked at was looking for a Bible teacher for high school boys. The thought of teaching in a Christian school seemed like something too good to be true. I would teach high school kids about the Bible. No board meetings, no budget to manage, no recruiting people to serve in ministry, and no constant problems to deal with. Was that really the issue that made me leave the pastoral ministry? At the time, I would have said it was, but upon retrospect and revelation, I have come to believe, it was what I did not know that really hurt me.

There are levels of competency in any vocation. I am sure you have already asked the question of your ministry, "Am I doing this right?" I know I did. We had the academic training, but when it comes to actually being a pastor, that involves practical application. It is one thing to read in a book how to have a good marriage, but it is something totally different to have a good marriage. The problem lies in the fact that we have not been married before and we have not developed the skills, or had the necessary experience. It only took me about 20 years to figure out some of the really dumb things I was doing in my marriage. After 48 years I am not sure my wife would say I am really competent at being a good husband, but she might say I have improved.

Being competent means having the knowledge, but also the skills and experience at doing something. Being incompetent means not having the knowledge, skills and experience. The first level of competency is unconscious incompetence. That is where most of us begin in ministry. This is the most difficult stage because we do not even know what we don't know. We may think we are competent, but in reality we are not. We dated our spouse and so we thought we were competent in relationships. This is a very difficult stage to pass through primarily because of stubbornness. We don't want to admit that we don't know what we are doing. The second stage is conscious incompetence. We come to the place where we realize maybe we really don't know what we need to know. It is not just a matter of doing something for a duration of time. We may have been a pastor for 15-20 years, but that does not mean we have that many years of experience. As John Maxwell says, "You have 1 year of experience 15-20 times." It is at the point of conscious incompetence we are willing to try and figure out what it is that we don't know. We begin to search for answers. We read books, talk to people with experience and work at becoming competent. Perhaps this is where you are now. The third stage is being consciously competent. At this point we know what to do, but we need to think about it to be competent. The last stage is unconscious competence. You are unconscious again! But this time, you are unconscious about your competence. Everything you've learned, experienced, and mastered, is just second nature to you now. Once you reach this level, the final one, you do everything the right way without even thinking about it. I am writing under the assumption that you are, as I was, in stage 1 or 2. The plan is to get to stage 3. From there, you can work on stage 4. Perhaps, if I had known and been in stage 3, I would have been more effective and experienced greater satisfaction.

In leaving the pastoral ministry I do not think I have forsaken God, and he certainly has not forsaken me. I do not think I am currently operating outside of the will of God for my life. If you are reading this and have found yourself no longer pastoring, and wondering about your relationship with Christ because of that, I want you to know God doesn't abandon his children. He can use what you have experienced. The old saying is true: "You can't go back and make a new beginning, but you can begin today to make a new end." I look at my life and I have been a Christian for close to a half century. From the time I first sensed God's call on my life until where I am now has been almost exactly 40 years. It took Israel 40 years to get to the Promised Land, and it has taken me the same amount of time to get to where I am today. Neither Israel nor myself have been fast learners. However, that does not mean things could not have been different for me. I believe I have learned some things that had I known them earlier could have meant I would still be a pastor. My desire is to share some of those things with you. I do not want you to wake up one day and wonder, what happened?

SURVIVAL TIP #2

*Be Careful of to
Whom You Listen*

M any years ago, as I sat in a doctor's' office, I picked up a copy of "Field and Stream Magazine." As I browsed through the pages, I came across an article at the end of the magazine that was rather humorous. The author was writing on survival tips. And in particular, he was discussing what to do when you get lost in the woods. He began by telling what all of the experts say you should or shouldn't do in such an emergency. I thought it was interesting that he pointed out that the experts had not ever been lost. It is easy to say what not to do in a crisis if you have never been in that crisis. One of the many things the experts said you should not do, as a matter of fact, the number one thing you should not do, when you are lost in the woods, is do not panic. However, the author said he disagreed, and said that the very first thing that you should do is panic. He thought it would be helpful to give some advice on the most effective methods of panic. He began by giving three different types of panic. The first was something like just simply crying like a baby. The second became a little more involved. He recommended something that would resembled running around in circles screaming. However, he believed that the third type of panic might be the most beneficial. He gave it a name that was worthy of full scale panic. I don't recall his description, but for the sake of argument, we will call it full blown linear panic. This was panic where you started running as fast as you can, and screaming as loud as you can. He said he knew a fella who had practiced this form of panic and literally ran out of the woods, through a lumberjack camp and into civilization.

I am not sure that this is the best advice. It does remind me however of some of the advice we are given as pastors. Usually, we are told how to succeed by people who have succeeded. They attribute their success to the various programs that they have used in their ministry. However, I think I have tried just about every one of those programs, just as I am sure many of you have also. Unfortunately, my results were not the same as the guy who wrote that book or gave that seminar. Again, I wonder if this doesn't go back to the idea of competency. Several years ago I worked as a maintenance supervisor at a nursing home. One of the things I needed to be able to work on was air conditioners. They had 20 ton units with dual compressors and more little widgets and goes-on-to's than you can imagine. What

I needed to learn first was how to work on simple 3 ton units. When it came to ministry, much of what I seemed to read about was how to work on the 20 ton church, when I needed to know first how to work with a 3 ton church. Perhaps your church is more along the line of the 3 ton model, rather than the 20 ton behemoth unit.

One of the subjects I currently teach is inductive Bible study. The greatest difference between inductive and deductive study has to do with how you approach the Scriptures. In deductive study, you come with the answer and prove it from the Scripture. With inductive study, you come and ask questions: what is there, and then allow the Scriptures to tell you what is there. Deductive study is dogmatic and inductive study is open. The deductive study person would tell you what the Scripture means. Whereas, the inductive study person would tell you, "From what I have observed it could mean this." I don't know the specifics on what the problem is with your frustration and disappointment, but I can tell you that I have observed certain things and it could mean this. With that, allow me to share my observations, and leave you to your own interpretation.

We all would like to be able to read the definitive works on how to succeed in ministry wherever you are. That work has not been written. I am sure that we all desire to feel like we have succeeded. I will tell you that I know what it is to not get the desired outcome that would make me feel as though I had succeeded. There is no attempt here at trying to place blame on anyone or anything. We come to ministry with altruistic motives, but that does not guarantee success. One of my real failures had to do with the fact I did not know the meaning of success. I thought I had failed. I had used what others had set as the standard from which to measure my success----which is entirely arbitrary. I looked around at the lack of numerical growth and that appeared to me to be failure, but it was not failure at all. There was success, but I did not recognize it as success because the paradigm of success had come from others.

I have been running 3 miles, approximately three to five times a week, for more than 20 years. I do not run very fast. As a matter of fact, people pass me quite regularly. Now, I could gauge my success in running by whether or not I was able to run as fast or as long as other people. That would be very discouraging. I recall one instance where I ran on a track that was laid out in the shape of an 'L.' It was 5 o'clock in the morning so it was still dark when I ran. I remember running up behind a young lady who appeared to be in her 20's, and I passed her like she was going backwards. As I did, I thought to myself, man you are something else. You are a real stud. I was feeling pretty good about myself. As I came around the track I could look across the track and see the young lady I had just passed. To my ego upsetting surprise I saw a woman who looked to be approximately 8 to 9 months pregnant. So, maybe I'm not a stud. I don't gauge my running by what others are doing. I am out there doing it in the heat, cold and rain. I have been doing it for a long time. I may slow down more, but I will still be out there doing it. I have been asked if I have run a marathon. I say, "Yes, just about every two weeks."

I can look at what "successful" pastors have done and determine that I have been a failure. They have larger churches, bigger budgets, staff and the recognition of superiors. The apostle Paul wrote to his son in the Lord, Timothy in 2 Timothy 4:7 "I have fought the good fight, I have finished the race, I have kept the faith. Henceforth there is laid up for me the crown of righteousness, which the Lord, the righteous judge, will award to me on that day, and not only to me, but also to all who have loved his appearing. " Did you noticed that the apostle did not say that he had been successful. He does not mention the many people that have come to know Jesus because of what he had done. He does not mention the churches that he had planted. Yet, he says there is a crown awaiting him. He simply says that he has run the race and that he has been faithful. You and I will never be another Apostle Paul, but we can all be faithful. The size of your church, the number of members you have, the size of your annual budget or the number of people you have baptized does not determine your success. When you think about it, as one pastor said, "Everyone has their own score card on how successful you are. One person thinks it is how many people you have in attendance. Another thinks it is how many ministries you have going on in the church. For someone else, it is how many hospital visits you make." Success is running the race faithfully that counts. I will return to this later.

I would not presume to tell you that your church cannot grow numerically. I would seriously hope it will. I would not tell you that you should simply fold your hands and quit trying to do everything possible for that to happen, because we want to see people come to Christ and the Kingdom of God enlarged. I do not know how things are at your church. You may be busting out of the walls and looking to build a new multi-purpose facility. The one thing I do know is that is not the scenario for the majority of pastors in the United States. Reggie McNeal, in his book, "The Present Future," describes how the church has created "An entire industry...to help churches do whatever it is they decide to do. Consultants, para-church ministries, denominational headquarters, and publishing houses prod and push the church toward whatever the current fad is. A spate of program fixes have consistently over promised and under delivered. The suggestions are plentiful: offer small groups, contemporize your worship, market your services, focus on customer service, create a spiritual experience, become seeker-friendly, create a high expectation member culture, purify the church from bad doctrine, return to the basics. After decades of this kind of environment no wonder church leaders are a little skeptical about the 'next thing' and why many feel that just about the time they catch up they fall further behind. But the mailings keep coming, the seminars keep filling up, and the conference notebooks keep stacking up on the shelves." Are all those things good and helpful? Sure, but I would tell you to stop being obsessed with numerical growth and trying to be missional. It seems like we have become obsessed with numbers. I read an article that asked, "When did all the preachers become statistics junkies?" When was the last church leadership book you read or seminar you attended that didn't emphasize the value of setting goals for your church, then using some kind of metric to determine whether-or-not you were succeeding at reaching them. Again, goals are good because we need them to grow, but don't focus on numerical goals; focus on personal goals. Work first on yourself. Work most on yourself.

In a report on church size of major denominations across America, churches of under 100 make up 70% of the churches. When you look at churches of 50 or less the percentage is 40%. Going to the other end of the spectrum, churches of 500 only make up .3% of the churches in America. The percentages drop off significantly after 100 into the single digits.

There certainly is a need to assess progress. If we don't know how we're doing, how will we know if we are progressing? What truly is terribly wrong, is the trying to measure a church's success by using numbers. The things of greatest value are often immeasurable.

That same report, went on to address, that as pastors and leaders in what would be considered small churches, there is a need to realize that much of what works for larger churches doesn't necessarily work for smaller churches. The larger churches have the personnel, resources and culture that the smaller church does not have.

If you want to find out how well your church is doing, try this novel approach. Ask the people you minister to what they think. Make it so people know they can truly be honest with you; then sit down with them over a cup of coffee and ask them what they think, what they see and what they feel. Don't ask the person that complains all the time about everything. You know what they're going to say. The same goes for your biggest fan. Don't ask them; they will tell you how great things are.

Concentrate your efforts on two types of people. Talk to the people who have some emotional and spiritual maturity, but who don't offer their opinion very often. On the other end, sit down and have a conversation with younger people, new believers and to people who may not be believer's yet, but are attending your church. Let them know you're truly wanting their honest opinion.

In one study of several major denominations, churches with attendance in Sunday morning worship of 25-50 comprised of approximately 90% of churches. Yet, the men and women pastoring these churches have been made to feel like they are not as successful as the 10% that have more than that in attendance. Is the mother who raises 6 children more successful than the mother who raises 2?

I was reading an article by Dr. Charles Crow entitled "Understanding Church Culture and Behavior," and church growth and culture have been passions of his for many years. He has conducted extensive studies in this field. In the article he states, "For the most part, churches appear to reach the general size they will remain within the first five years of their founding. Many have reached that size by their second year and remain very close to that same size for long periods of time. " Go back in the records and history of your church and see how long it has been running about the same numbers. He goes on to quote Dr. Bill Sullivan who said "If they are staying about the same size over a long period of time the reason must be located in their culture or their paradigms. Virtually every church loses people every year. They must know how to find and take in new people or they would be getting smaller. Apparently, what they don't know how to do is change. " This is a topic for another chapter. The point being, that if your church has not grown numerically, that does not mean you are not successful. It may be there is something you don't know yet.

Someone has said, "Being a pastor is like being a high school football coach." Being a high school football coach means you must make a team. You must make a team from the players that you have. If you do not have a quarterback who is an effective passer you do not call pass plays. If you have a 145 pound running back, you don't call plays that call for him to run up the middle. Being a high school football coach means, what you are trying to do is to develop the boys and become a team. Too often, we think it's about the game. It is not about the game; it is about developing the team. I recently read an article about a football player who was going to play in the Senior Bowl. He was an All American safety. He had attended Ohio State University, but left there because the coach left. He went to Duke University. When asked about the coach, he said he was a good coach, but a better man. I don't know how many games the team won while he was there, but I can tell you that the coach developed a young man, and they were a team.

Today, there is a great deal of emphasis on being mis-sional. We think that it is our mission to reach the world for Jesus. Please do not misinterpret what I am saying. We desperately need to reach people for Christ. But as pastors, our first mission, is to make the team we have a people of Christian character. There has been much said in recent years about finding a need and meeting that need with a ministry. In the book, "Freedom for Ministry," the author says, "For a less demeaning and more distinctive ministry, we need to shift the metaphor from the meeting of human needs to the formation and sustaining of Christian charac-ter." We could restate that by saying, we need to shift the metaphor from being missional or evangelistic to the for-mation and sustaining of Christian character. I know that doesn't sound very trendy, but think about what character would mean for your congregation. Character implies the courage and grace to live the good life in a world where it is in desperate need of seeing such grace. The language of character has fallen into disuse in our culture. It is not trendy and sounds too old fashioned. We still speak of someone being 'a real character,' but that has a different and very limited connotation. The concept of character has a revered place in the Christian tradition, however, and is closely associated with notions such as virtue, re-sponsibility, honor, and obligation. In current understand-ings, character has little to do with what we have seen as vital to ministry, and that is a measure of how thoroughly those things have become captive to secular thinking of what ministry should be. Eugene Peterson, in his book,

"The Unnecessary Pastor," writes, "The overriding concern in the Pastoral Epistles is in 'healthy' or 'sound' teaching. Eight times in all these three letters we find concern for the 'health of teaching or words.' Sometimes 'teaching' is translated 'doctrine' and so we get the impression that orthodoxy is at issue. But this isn't quite right. For the Apostle Paul gives Timothy a mandate to teach in a way that brings health to people." I would say that fairly accurately describes what pastoral responsibility is meant to be.

As I have sat and listened to my pastor preach, I realize he is a phenomenal speaker. However, it occurred to me that he is more than a good preacher; he is a very good pastor too. It is not his oratory skills that make him a good pastor. What makes him a good pastor is he works at forming and sustaining Christian character in his people. Think about it. What kind of questions do pastors ask each other when they come together in meetings? They are questions like: "How is your church doing?" "How is your Sunday School doing?" "How is this ministry or that ministry doing?" When you think about it, these are the same questions of denominational reports. Is ministry really about how we keep score and determine champions, division leaders, and losers. What if, instead, we asked about people, not the institution? What if church leaders asked each other, "How is God at work in your people? Or "Where do you see Jesus bustin' out?" That is a complete change in thinking about our responsibility as leaders.

I think it is instructive to read what A.W. Tozer said. This is a man who died in 1963, yet what he said sounds like he could be speaking to us in the 21st century. He said, "Oh, brother or sister, God calls us to worship, but in many instances we are in entertainment, just running a poor second to the theaters. That is where we are, even in evangelical churches, and I don't mind telling you that most of the people we say we are trying to reach will never come to a church to see a lot of amateur actors putting on a home talent show. Now in our town we have a huge church that has the finest musicians and all of the professional trappings to draw a crowd, but I would guess your church probably does not have such luxuries. People who will come to your church will come to hear their granddaughter sing, or they will come because they like the grandparents of the girl singing the special. When my granddaughter was 12 she played the piano and sang in church; she probably would not win on "American Idol," but I was blessed by it. I would rather hear her sing than a famous gospel singer. I would say, "Stop trying to appeal to the people who will not come to your church and seek to minister to the people who already come to your church."

When we don't know what we don't know and think we do know, we create problems. We come out of school with all this amazing knowledge we have gained and we come thinking we know what needs to be done to get the church growing. Don't you just hate it when you have been working on some project for awhile, and it isn't going as planned? Then someone comes along, who knows absolutely nothing about what you have done or what problems you have encountered, and they proceed to tell you how to get it right. How would you feel if I came into your church and told you that everything you were doing was wrong? Would you feel defensive? Would you feel resentful? Of course you would. That is what I did with the churches I pastored. Oh, I didn't come in and act critical, and I didn't say those words, but I told them what we need to do to grow, and what needed to happen for the church to be what God wanted it to be. What that said to them was, "You aren't what God wants you to be, and all you have been doing is wrong." Now, I know you wouldn't have done that when you came to your church. You wouldn't try to institute new programs and wide sweeping changes from the way they had been doing things for the last twenty years, but I did. So many churches have had several pastors, and every one of them has come and told them how they need to change. When I came, I was in a line of pastors who all said the same thing. I was so fortunate to have people who went along with me, but going along and really buying in is two different things. They would do what was asked of them, but they were not committed to what was being done. I remember saying we needed to have a mission statement. Every good organization (translated, successful organization) has to have a mission statement, and that goes for the church? What is a mission statement without core values? We also needed a set of core values. We put them on big boards where they would be seen as soon as you came in the church. Did people become more evangelistic, compassionate, caring or generous? Were they totally committed to the mission statement and core

CONVERSATIONS ON PASTORIAL SURVIVAL

values statement? No. They were merely statements put on boards for people to see.

I gave the church my resignation in March, telling them that the last Sunday in June would be my last Sunday. By April they had already taken the mission statement and core values down from the walls. Why? It was not really their mission statement or core values, but mine. Are mission statements and core values important? Absolutely. However, telling people doesn't make them change. If we want to see real, lasting change occur in the church we will first need to model the way. Do consistently, over a long period of time, what you want done by others.

As I have reflected on ministry I wondered, where do pastors succeed? In small places. I recently heard a story from a pastor who received in the mail 5 one dollar bills, with a note attached. The note was from a woman who said she had just been paid $50 for cleaning a house; the $5's was the first time she had ever tithed. That is being successful. It's the story I heard about a man who had rheumatoid arthritis. When the pastor first came to the church this man could barely walk. Before the pastor left the church, that same man was confined to a wheelchair having both legs amputated. In constant pain, he often sat at his dining room table asleep because he was so drugged to alleviate his pain. One evening the pastor received a call that the man had fallen while his wife was trying to get him in bed. His wife couldn't lift him, and called the pastor to come help. The man couldn't help the pastor in trying to get him up. He was dead weight, and without legs weighed as much as the pastor weighed. They got him in the bed and he was in tremendous pain. That pastor crawled up on the bed and put his arms around him and wept with him, prayed for him, and kissed him on the cheek and left. That was being a pastor. That was being successful. He relayed that years later he was told how that moment impacted those who witnessed it.

I did not recognize success. But, years after leaving my last church I was asked to come back and conduct 3 funerals. When families want you to be the one to say the final words concerning their loved ones you have succeeded. The most important thing we can do is love the people God has given us and make them a team, forming and sustaining Christian character in them. It is not about the game. When we really love our people and do not see them as tools, and they come to know we love them, we will be successes. Someone said, and I believe it to be true, you will be more successful by going to a football game of one of the young people in your church, or by sitting at the dinner table of one of your families, than you ever will from your preaching and the time you spend in your study. People will more than gladly tolerate mediocre preaching from a pastor who they know loves them. By the same token, they will not tolerate a pastor who doesn't genuinely love them even though he is the greatest orator. Lloyd Douglas is quoted in Norman Shawchuck's book "Leading the Congregation: Caring for Yourself While Serving the People, "If it comes to pass that by industry, application, and the proper use of your talents, you should become a ranking member of your profession, known far and wide...so be it. If that never comes to pass, and you spend your ministry merely going about doing good, your name unknown except to those whose hearts you have touched by personal contact, you may find satisfaction in remembering that many there be who have no memorial; who perished as though they had never been; but their righteousness hath not been forgotten, and the honor of their deeds cannot be blotted out." The questions are: do I want the church to bless me, or do I want to bless them? Do I want the church to enrich my life, or do I want to enrich their lives? That is what it means to bless. When I was ordained in the Church of God, at the installation service I was asked if there was any particular hymn I would like sung. One pastor at the installation would remind me and laugh at my selection when we met at other functions. The song, "Little is Much if God is in it." The chorus says, "Little is much if God is in it. Labor not for wealth or fame. There's a crown and you can win it, if you'll go in Jesus' name." I still think the words are true.

When we talk about Christianity and what the Bible says, we know that it is all about relationship. It is about our relationship with Christ and our relationship with one another. The same is true when it comes to being a pastor. We come to a new church and we believe this is going to be a great experience. We have all kinds of visions of the future. For the first six months we enjoy what is commonly referred to as "the honeymoon." Then reality sinks in and the people are not all we thought they were, and somehow we need to change them. How appropriate that we refer to that period as "the honeymoon." It is just like a marriage. We got married to the perfect woman or she thought the perfect man. Shortly after, normal life kicked in and there were all kinds of things that were less than ideal. That is when we start to try and change that person. As I said earlier, I have been married to Barbara for 48 years and about 20 years into marriage I made an amazing discovery. I found that if I would focus on trying to make her happy instead of trying to make her make me happy, she would reciprocate. I am not advocating that you try to make your church happy by just letting them do anything they want. But, when they called you they were hoping they were calling someone who would genuinely love them for who they were, and enrich and bless their lives, and not someone who wanted them for what they could do to advance your ministerial career. If we will do that, they will break their necks trying to do all that will advance your career.

Please allow another analogy from me. I have loved doing carpentry and cabinetry. I have built much of the furniture in my home, as well as in the homes of my children. I get a great deal of satisfaction out of seeing the finished product. There is a sense of accomplishment to be able to stand back and look at what you have done and admire it. It is very tangible because you can see and touch it. I think that is what we want in ministry. We want to see something happen. I am reminded of the story of the lumberjack who was hired, at $50 an hour, to take the blunt part of his axe and hit a log all day. At the end of the day he quit. He was told that he would be paid $100 an hour if he would come back and continue to hit the log. He refused, saying, "I can't do that. I have to see chips fly when I chop wood." We are the same way. We want to see something happen. Jesus said if we would give a glass of water in his name we have done it unto him. A glass of water will not make a noticeable difference. My wife cooks supper for me every evening. Each meal doesn't seem to make much of a difference in my life, unless I eat too much. Then, it begins to show in a somewhat less than pleasant way. But I need those suppers to be nourished and strengthened for another day. We may not see much happening in the church we pastor, but we feed the people every week good food from the word of God. We help them through the difficult times in their lives. And, while every meal doesn't make a drastic change in them; the kinds of changes we would like to see; they needed the meal just the same. Therefore, the second survival tip is to be careful to whom you listen. Being successful is building your team and instilling in them Christian character. You will do that by consistently feeding them the word of God and loving them.

Dawn, M. & Peterson, E. (2000) The Unnecessary Pastor. Grand Rapids, Mich. Wm B. Eerdmanns Pub.

Douglas, L., Shawchuck, N. (1993). Leading the Congregation: Caring for Yourself While Serving the People. Nashville, Tenn. Abingdon Press.

McNeal, R. (2003). The Present Future. San Francisco, CA. Jossey Bass Pub.

Neuhaus, Richard. (1992). "Freedom for Ministry." Grand Rapids, Mich. Wm. B. Eerdmans Pub.

Tozer, A.W. Smith, G. ed. (1985)"Whatever happened to worship?" Camp Hill, Penn. Christian Publications

SURVIVAL TIP #3

Realize You are in Dangerous Territory

I really enjoyed the movie, "Kelly's Heroes," with Clint Eastwood, who leads the guys in his group behind enemy lines to get a huge pile of gold. They know they are in dangerous territory, but it doesn't always look dangerous. At one place they cross a plowed field, that looks like some farmer worked. About half way through the field one guy steps on a landmine and is killed. It didn't look like a dangerous place, but a man is killed. Ministry doesn't look like a dangerous place. After all, we are working in God's Church with God's people. What could possibly be dangerous about that? You're laughing, aren't you? But this is no laughing matter. After years as a pastor, I look around and the ground before me is littered with the fatalities of ministry. Many of the men and women I went to college with are no longer in ministry, and I had to come to grips with my own sense of no longer being a pastor.

I recently tried to replace the battery in my cell phone. In the old days it was a matter of popping off the back, slipping the old battery out and the new battery in, and snapping the back on. Not anymore. Needless to say, once I got the phone back together it didn't work. I took it to a place called something like "We Fix It". When I went to pick it up the prognosis was my phone had given up the ghost and it was unfixable. I was looking at having to buy another $650 phone. This was particularly bad since I had just bought that phone, having dropped my previous phone in the toilet. Are you getting the picture here? This isn't just bad, it is terrible. But then I found out I had insurance on this phone and all of a sudden my problem was fixable, and I would get another phone for $168. That which sounded terrible earlier and my problem being unfixable, went to still being a problem, but it was one that was fixable. Keep that in mind as you read the following statistics. At first, things sometimes look unbelievably bad. Then, you learn they are still bad, but not unmanageable.

Every day, there are many that are leaving the ministry and I believe there are reasons that could be mitigated, so I began my investigation of why men and women leave ministry. Consider the following statistics on ministerial dissatisfaction and decide if this is in deed dangerous territory: According to an article from *Pastor Appreciation*, figures stated that 1500 pastors quit churches every month. There is no single reason for this, but I believe that many leave because of relational difficulties in the church. Certainly, there are toxic churches that are capable of chewing up pastors and spitting them out with great regularity. And it only takes a few antagonists to cause substantial havoc and devastation. If we are unable to get along with the leadership of the church, we can be sure we will experience frustration and disappointment. Those leaders will make sure of that. One report indicated that 41 percent of congregations who fired their pastor had done so at least twice before. Guy Greenfield, in his book *The Wounded Minister* said, "In my own denomination (Southern Baptist), it has regularly been reported that between 2000 and 2500 ministers are forced out of the ministry each year. Other denominations as well as independent churches are reporting similar problems of significant magnitude." G. Lloyd Rediger writes in *Clergy Killers*, "One informed estimate indicates that a pastor is fired (Forced out) every six minutes in the United States".

"Research conducted by the Barna Group, The Alban Institute, Duke University, H.B. London, The Fuller Institute, among a host of others, continues to reveal both the nature of the problem and the source. A 1994 study of 4300 Protestant clergy, found that thirty-two percent of female clergy and twenty-eight percent of male clergy said they had contemplated leaving the ministry in the past year. In another similar survey, it was found that fifty percent of those currently serving as clergy had considered leaving the ministry within the last 3 months. The other fifty percent of the pastors, who responded, reported being so discouraged that they would leave the ministry immediately if they could, but had no other way of making a living. Eighty percent of seminary graduates who enter the ministry will leave the ministry within the first five years of serving the church. Eighty-five percent of pastors said their greatest problem is they are 'sick and tired of dealing with problem people, such as disgruntled elders, deacons, worship leaders, worship teams, board members, and associate pastors.' Ninety percent of pastors said the hardest thing about ministry is dealing with uncooperative people. Nationally, for every ten young people in their 20's who graduates from seminary and enters full time ministry, only one in ten will still be in ministry at retirement age."

It has been documented that "Cardiovascular disorder, cancer, arthritis, gastrointestinal disorders, and respiratory problems used to be rare among clergy, and once generated the best mental health and longevity statistics of any profession. Not anymore!" One writer, referring to clergy, states, that while at one time, clergy were an insurers dream, this is no longer the case. Clergy now generate statistics and actuarial data similar to the general public.

Whew! You made it through all those horrible statistics that might lead you to believe that the problem with ministry is not fixable. I was deeply disturbed by those statistics, but I was not shocked. But then I found some things that convinced me that the problem is not unfixable. If we look closely at the major causes for pastors leaving the ministry we see that the problem is not terminal. Our greatest problems come from working with people. I am sure that comes as no surprise to you. I thought I was on to a solution. I suggested that when someone came to the altar for salvation, we could inquire as to their assurance of salvation. If they said they were sure if they died they would go to heaven, we could kill them right there. That would eliminate them backsliding (if you believe in that), and they would never cause trouble in the church. I could never get agreement on my solution. I do believe there are real, substantive answers on how to effectively and productively work and relate to the people we serve. I do not believe the problems are all a matter of sinful, carnal parishioners. I do not believe you have to be part of those statistics.

If you investigate how this problem had been handled in the past at the denominational level, you might come to the conclusion that this must not be a very serious issue. This only exacerbated the problem because there appeared to be little concern at the leadership level for this devastation on ministers, their families, as well as the damage inflicted upon the mission and spiritual energy of the congregations where ministers leave. It often seemed like the attitude was that if men and women are truly called of God then nothing will so discourage them as to make them quit. I read that one seminarian recalled that at the seminary he attended, 90 percent of the curriculum was devoted to content, 10 percent focused on skill, and our character and ethics, but how we lived in relationship with others was never addressed beyond a few talks in chapel. It was assumed that who we are as people and how we related to others had been addressed prior to our arrival at seminary. I do not recall anything related to personality dysfunction being mentioned when I went through Bible college. The focus was academics and how well we did on a paper or exam. I do think that attitude has changed and there is greater concern for pastors.

The role of the pastor is probably one of the most stressful of all roles, and very few people are ideally suited for the task. It is a task that requires an abundance of grace to adequately fulfill. I like what Dan Allender said about being a minister. He writes, "So here's the truth: if you're a leader, you're in the battle of your life. Nothing comes easily, enemies outnumber allies, and the terrain keeps shifting under your feet." This is dangerous territory. That is not a reflection upon the people with whom we work, but the further up in leadership you go the larger the target gets on your back for the enemy to attack. Remember, as the Apostle Paul wrote, "We battle not flesh and blood, but powers and principalities in high places." And, as he alludes to, how to play the game keeps changing with the changing of culture. Technology is moving so quickly that it is difficult to keep up with. We have gone from modernism to post-modernism, and who knows what is just ahead. Yet, the greatest challenge will continue to be how to effectively relate to the people we are trying to lead. This survival tip accentuates the need for making sure we learn every tip we can to survive. In the next chapters I will attempt to outline some helpful tips on how to survive pastoral ministry. Like any sermon outline it will be up to you to flesh it out.

Allender, D. (2006). "Leading With A Limp". Colorado Springs, Co. Waterbrook Press

Ask Our Staff, "Why Are So Many Pastors Leaving The Ministry," www.parsonage.org/ (accessed May 10, 2010).

Goetz, D. "Forced Out," *Christianity Today*, January 1, 1996, www.christianitytoday.com/ le/1996/winter/611040.html. (accessed May 10,2010).

Greenfield,G. (2005). *The Wounded Minister*.Grand Rapids, Mich. Baker Books

Rediger, G. Loyd. (1997). *Clergy Killers*. Louisville, Ky. Westminster John Knox Press,

Slater, P. *"The Relationship Of Pastors Leaving The Ministry With The Lack Of Pastor Appreciation And Career Change For Pastors,"* *Pastor Appreciation.net*, www.pastor-appreciation.net/ (accessed May 10, 2010).

SURVIVAL TIP #4
Be Aware of Your Closest Enemy

I can be absorbed for hours reading history, and I particularly like Civil War history. I have had the privilege to visit some of the Civil War battle fields. The people of that era are extremely interesting. One person stands out from the crowd. His name is Abraham Lincoln; probably the greatest president this nation has ever been fortunate to have. He is still being quoted today for he was a man of tremendous insight. He said, "America will never be destroyed from the outside. If we falter and lose our freedoms, it will be because we destroyed ourselves." I think that while this is true about America, as a nation, I think it is equally true to a large degree about pastoral ministry. If ministry is destroyed it probably won't come from outside. We are more likely to fail because we have destroyed ourselves.

We have all heard of the church scandal, and right away we think of some immoral or illegal scenario like the pastor embezzling funds, or having an affair with the church secretary. However, the word scandal is the Greek word *"scandalon."* It means trap-spring, stumbling block, a cause of ruin, destruction, or misery. It is actually that little thing on a mousetrap that triggers the trap to slam down, breaking the neck of the poor, little, defenseless mouse. There are some things that are traps for the pastor. This has also commonly been referred to as, "the dark side of leadership." To me, that sounds too much like "Star Wars," and Darth Vader, who represents the evil side. But, there are traps, and they are traps because the pastor is not aware of them. We may realize there is something wrong, but too often, we attribute it to the people in the congregation, rather than to something much closer.

I recently read an illustration where a baby is placed on the floor. He has not learned how to crawl yet, but he can push himself backwards. He begins to do so, and eventually backs himself in between a table and chair, where he hits his head. After repeated bumps the baby thinks the problem is the chair. Thrashing about, crying and banging his head on the furniture, he is stuck and hates it. So what does he do? He pushes harder, which only makes the problem worse. If he could talk, he would blame the furniture. This makes sense because, after all, he is doing everything he knows to do. You and I know that the problem is not the furniture, but he is the problem. Unfortunately, he can't see that. We do the same thing. We blame everything else for our problems, when in fact, we are the problem. As the cartoon character Pogo said, "We have seen the enemy, and he is us." This goes back to stage one of competency. We don't know, but more importantly, we don't know that we don't know. Being cognizant of the traps means we can do something to minimize being caught in them. We need to find out where the traps are. What are those things that are catching us by surprise? What are we banging our heads on, while blaming other things for our problems?

Phillip Gulley is a Friends pastor and has a series of books about life in the little community and church he pastored. He describes people and events, and I do not know if the people are real or fictional, but I would read his books and be thoroughly entertained with his colorful description of the way some people acted. Immediately, my mind would flash to my current church or a previous church. I would think, "I have a person just like that in my church." Or, "They remind me of someone I have pastored." I believe I could relate a story about some precious soul in one of my assignments and you would nod your head, because you have had, or even have right now, someone just like that in your church. You love them, but they are a source of difficulty. Tennessee Ernie Ford would say, "Bless their little pea pickin' hearts." Sometimes, when they leave the church you might say, "Everyone is a blessing. Some bless you by coming and others bless you by leaving." The truth is, there are some congregations that say the same thing about their pastors.

There are some people who are clinically dysfunctional. That is, they are in need of serious professional help. They have problems relating in a healthy way to others. They have trouble relating to their family, their co-workers and to people in the church. They are Christians, and they may tithe and attend regularly. There are others, in the church, who are dysfunctional, but they are able to relate to others without causing serious problems. However, their dysfunction is still a source of relational difficulty. They may even be on the church board. They are often in leadership roles. One such person in your church like that may likely be you. Reggie McNeal says, "I see some unhealthy caregivers in ministry who are often so needy for approval themselves that they allow their boundaries to be violated by church members, then wind up bitter toward the people they are serving. They refuse to release ministry to laypeople because they would then lose their own identity. They complain about how they are overworked, mistreated, and unappreciated. Their sense of entitlement betrays them. Some are controllers who search for status under the guise of being caring servants. Some have entered ministry largely for their own needs and then complain when those aren't being met." Does any of that sound disturbingly familiar? Would members use any of those descriptions of you?

Consequently, it is critical to address the emotional health of the pastor. In the past, we have assumed that once a person became a Christian and they were Spirit filled, that took care of relational problems. If there were relational problems, they were just a result of the sinful nature. We acted as if a person was saved, sanctified, and called to ministry, fulfilled the required educational material, then they were qualified to pastor. Denominations are coming to realize that many of the people who graduate from their universities and seminaries are going into the ministry with baggage that, instead of being a source of help, are a hindrance to the health of the church.

John Calvin said, "Without knowledge of self, there is no knowledge of God." We need to investigate if we could be the source of relational problems that are plaguing our ministry. Pastor Peter Scazzero, pastor of New Life Fellowship in Queens, New York, and author of "The Emotionally Healthy Church," wrote, "With all my background in prayer and the Bible, it was quite a shock to realize that whole layers of my life existed that God had not yet touched." Part of the problem is we are unaware of our own inner turmoil.

We are like icebergs, in that only about 10% of who we are is seen by others. There is another 90% that goes unseen. What is seen however, are the effects of that 90%. The late secretary of the United Nations, Dag Hammarskjold said, "The longest journey of any person is the journey inward." The work of change must start at the top and not at the bottom. That is true whether we are talking about changing a nation, a church or a ministry. Everything rises and falls on leadership. As the leader goes, so goes the church. When we are willing to do the hard work of becoming an emotionally and spiritually mature disciple of Jesus Christ, their will be a ripple effect that will impact everyone within your sphere of influence. For many, that is a scary journey. But we need not fear looking within, because God sees the 90% that is hidden and he utterly and completely loves us. It does not mean we are less Christian or less called of God. You are not the problem. In the words of psychiatrist, Dr. Gregory Khory, "The problem is the problem." We only need to look at some of the people called in the Bible to see God called some people who had issues. However, we all have weaknesses that can contribute to failure. The reason we need to look at our own personal dysfunction or dark side is, "To the degree you attempt to hide or dissemble your weaknesses, the more you will need to control those you lead, the more insecure you will become, and the more rigidity you will impose—prompting the ultimate departure of your best people." Revealing is the beginning of healing. We are seriously hindered from helping others when we are in need of help ourselves.

Before going any further I have to tell you that I am operating on four assumptions from Gary MacIntosh's book "Overcoming the Dark Side of Leadership."

First, I would say that every leader suffers from some degree of dysfunction, varying from mild to extreme. As a matter of fact, all of God's children suffer from some form of dysfunction. Everyone since Adam and Eve has been dysfunctional, because we do not function as we were initially designed to function. The difference is in how much it affects our relationships with others. Unfortunately, we are so joined to who people think we are that we are not willing to come to acknowledge just how messed up we are. In reality, people really don't think we have it all together, as much as we think they do. They too, experience our dysfunction. We leave them shaking their heads wondering, "What is wrong with them?" Again, I will say, you are not the problem, the problem is the problem.

Secondly, many leaders are unaware of the dysfunctional part of their personalities that drives them. I am obsessive compulsive and I couldn't understand what was wrong with everyone else. Why isn't everyone like me? I thought people were lazy and were not conscientious. I thought that if you want something done right, you do it yourself. I was critical and controlling. I drove people nuts with new ideas and the pressure to do whatever needed to be done. It also meant I had bulldog tenacity. Once I got an idea in my head there was no getting rid of that idea, until it became a reality. The bulldog has an upturned nose so it can continue to breathe once it latches on to its prey. I don't have an upturned nose, but I can be equally tenacious. I didn't know that this too was part of my dysfunction.

Third, learning about our dysfunction and what created it can enable us to address those areas, and prevent, or mitigate the potential negative effects to our leadership, while still realizing our great potential. This is necessary because our dysfunction keeps the church from being all it can be. It is just like a dysfunctional family member whose behavior causes everyone else in the family to act in a way as to not upset that member. It is the the story of the mother who is extremely overweight but nobody in the family can say anything about the continuous eating of pizza, cookies and ice cream because she gets angry and abusive. Nobody says anything because they don't want to upset her. We enable people to remain dysfunctional because we don't address their dysfunction. The alternatives are to avoid them or bring the dysfunction to light. People have enabled us to remain dysfunctional because it seems safer than saying anything. Often, it is chalked up to, "Oh, that's just the way they are."

Finally, Scripture has a great deal to say about dysfunctions in our personalities, which can be helpful for the leader to understand himself and overcome those areas that would threaten his ministry. We only have to look at the three patriarchs of the Old Testament to see the problem. Abraham was a liar and a coward. He lied about Sarah being his wife because he was afraid of being killed for her. Isaac, had to live with the fact that as a teenager his father was a split second from killing him. If God had not intervened, Isaac would have been killed. Jacob was so self-serving that he allowed his mother to help him deceive his father and to manipulate getting his brother's birthright. Yet, God used these people and they were an important part of his redemption plan for mankind. That means there is hope for us here in the 21st century. God is still using flawed creatures like you and me to reach a lost and dying world.

What is the catalyst for developing this dysfunction or dark side in our personality? How did we get this way?

When I was growing up, whenever I did something wrong I would get smacked on the back of the head by my father. Could that be my problem? I often use that as an excuse for doing dumb things, but I don't think that was a contributing factor. There are experiences and influences that come into our lives through childhood and adolescents that are instrumental in the creation of our dysfunction. Again, as Dan Allender says in his book, "Leading with a Limp," "We always predict the future by reading the present from a frame of reference that was established in the past." I have had people tell me that I am just like my father. I have discovered the lingering power of the family into which I was born. We leave those families when we leave home or get married, but we continue to be shaped by them. These dysfunctions are inner urges, compulsions, and motivations that either help us succeed or sabotage our efforts. It is not the result of some single event in our life, but the dysfunctions in our personality are built brick by brick, over a long period of time. There are sin patterns, passed on from generation to generation in our families, that are still operational in our lives. One study of 6000 men discovered that not one of them got "through adolescence without having at least one 'ranking session' with peers. The event had a variety of names at the time, but was typically a tense interchange of insults and putdowns, punctuated by laughter, best performed in front of a teenage audience that found it entertaining. We call some of that peer pressure. Children can be some of the cruelest people when it comes to someone else. We can all recall how the embarrassing moments in childhood were magnified. The spectators to our misery were especially inclined to giggle since it wasn't their egos that were taking a beating at that particular moment. In childhood we may have successfully learned how to effectively cope with a bad situation in the home by being an appeaser, rescuer, problem solver, or fighter, and because of our success, we began to rely on that approach to all conflicts. Even when that approach has not been successful we continued to depend on it. This has been called the "tyranny of successful habits."

As I have already alluded to, the amazing thing about some dysfunctional behavior is that it is also the driving force behind what makes many people successful. Norman Shawchuck, in his book, "Leading the Congregation," said, "For many the motivating forces that drive decisions and actions spring from spirits other than the Spirit of God." That does not mean to say that preachers are motivated by evil spirits, but there is "an 'internal theater' that strongly influences the character and quality of the leader's leadership." When we have had several bad experiences of the same or similar nature, we anticipate those same experiences to happen in other relationships. We have seen this before and expect bad things, even if that is not the reality. In one study, documented in "The Neurotic Organization," the researchers said, "Core themes in a leader's 'inner theater' cause him or her to choose certain courses of action, and these themes hold the key to success or failure of the leader." They go on to say, "Leaders can become prisoners of their internal psychic theater so that their actions become self-defeating." One writer of a secular book, entitled, "Ambitious Men," said, "The problems of powerful men are rarely simple; neither are the solutions. They struggle with such things as they aren't making as much money as others, being promoted quick enough. It can be they are not winning admiration as widely as they anticipated, or their own business isn't growing." May I inject here: When it comes to pastor's, the same things could be stated as: their church isn't growing, they aren't being paid as well as other pastors, they are not given the recognition by their congregations or state leaders. The writer goes on to say, "Their first impulse is to use the approach that worked before, this time more energetically. Should that too fail, they are willing to try a slight shift in direction. Through it all they remain convinced that their general strategy is still effective and that a minor course correction will result in significant improvement. They have good reason to think this, since the formula worked well enough to bring them to their present level of achievement." Those protective mechanisms used in childhood and adolescence are the same ones used in ministry. The problem is that they do not work, but we continue to use them.

Most Americans admired the late John F. Kennedy as a great president. But, he too, was terribly dysfunctional and had a dark side. In Ralph Martin's book "Seeds of Destruction," he says of John's father Joe, "He had a hot heart and a cold head, which created a special animal vigor, a boundless self-confidence, and an awesome ego. Yet no matter how handsome his various houses, no matter how powerful his government positions, people always saw him as a pushy outsider, a crass Catholic. All of this built up into growing resentment—Joe Kennedy would neither forget nor forgive—a resentment he passed on to his sons. It became the touchstone of his life".

As one of the richest men in the country, Kennedy decided that money had meaning only if it brought power. And the more power he got, the more he wanted. A United States Supreme Court Justice once said of him, "Isn't [he] the most evil man you ever met, the most evil of the entire lot"?

Joe's sons later demonstrated assorted degrees of his charm, vitality, and magnetism, yet they also showed some of his dark side." As others have noted, Joe taught his sons to win "at any cost, tailoring the truth to one's own advantage, and the privileges of money and power." He goes on to say, "John Kennedy's entire adult life was nothing more than a desperate attempt to gain the ever elusive approval of his father. Whether it manifested itself in his need to achieve during school years to his rapid ascent up the ladder of political power."

Before you start to think that this is something for the world, but not the ministry, let me relate a story about Bill Hybel, the pastor of Willow Creek Community Church. He pastors a large congregation in excess of 15,000 in attendance. When Bill was a boy he worked in his father's wholesale produce company. It was there that he learned that you stay at a task until it was completed, regardless of the demands physically or emotionally. One illustration he tells is about the day he had to empty a truckload of rotten potatoes. "After hours of unloading bag after bag of slimy, smelly potatoes, he complained to his father about the number of bags still remaining. 'Don't worry Billy,' his father said, 'you only have to unload them one at a time.'" That is how Bill faced life. No matter how hard the task was he stayed at it until every slimy, smelly bag was unloaded. We admire that type of fortitude and work ethic, but he became a workaholic where every hour of everyday was consumed unloading one bag after another. And you can imagine, with a church membership of 15,000, there were lots of bags; so many bags he could never get them all unloaded. He said, "One Saturday, just a few hours before the evening service and a few minutes before he was to officiate at a friend's wedding, I laid my head down on my desk and sobbed uncontrollably, entirely depleted of physical, emotional, and spiritual strength." This demonstrates that, whether we are talking about a beloved American president, an infamous world dictator, the CEO of a Fortune 500 company, a servant-minded pastor of a country church, or a prominent denominational leader, the dark side is indiscriminant when it comes to choosing its victims. It doesn't matter if it is a well-intentioned leader or a diabolical dictator, driven by sinister motives, their dark side, like oil in a body of water, will always find its way to the surface and create a mess if it is not acknowledged and redeemed.

Now we might be tempted to dismiss much of this as simply a part of being fallen creatures; just a flaw of being part of the human race. Before we do that we need to understand that the leader's dysfunction hinders the effectiveness of the organization. As Shawchuck reminds us, "The interior life of the leader, when ignored, can lead to disaster for the leader and the organization alike." When leaders lack the ability to make decisions, fail to inform people so they know what is expected of them or give proper feedback about their performance, it may cause political infighting by people who attempt to advance their own projects. Pessimism may pervade the organization and people procrastinate. People react to our dysfunction and seek to find ways to compensate for it. They may do so by leaving or avoiding ministry and working with the dysfunctional leader. Your church is a reflection of your leadership, and if you are dysfunctional, guess what, there is a good chance your church probably is as well. There are about 12 emotional problems in the *Diagnostic and Statistical Manual of Mental Disorders* that I personally identify with, but for this I have identified 5 personality dysfunctions that may shed some light on your dysfunction. They are: co-dependence, obsessive compulsive, narcissistic, paranoid, and passive aggressive.

Earlier, I said that to be a successful pastor you only need to love your people. If you are co-dependent you are too busy wanting them to love you. If you are obsessive, compulsive you are too busy getting people to get it together and having everything perfect. If you are narcissistic you are too busy loving yourself to love others. If you are paranoid, how can you love people you think are out to get you? And, if you are passive aggressive people are to be used, and when they don't respond you will sulk and isolate yourself, feeling sorry for yourself, rather than loving them.

I do not want to leave you here. I want to leave you with a positive note. The title of Dan Allender's book, "Leading with a Limp," caused me to think immediately of Jacob who wrestled with the Lord and ended up walking with a limp. He was forever reminded of his weakness, yet he was the father of a nation honored by God. Jacob certainly was dysfunctional, but God used him in a mighty way. To another dysfunctional man, Jesus said, "My grace is sufficient for you, for power is perfected in weakness." (2Cor.12:9) We need to realize that our ministry is often shaped as much by our weaknesses as by our strengths. That doesn't mean we should focus on our weaknesses. We need to run with our strengths and avoid those people and tasks that expose our weaknesses. Remember that the story of God is not about human potential; it is the revelation of the kindness and passion of the Father.

I think it is important to point out that our dysfunction is not because we were born this way, or that we are bad people. It is not a matter of trying to place blame. However, like making a cake, we are very much a product of what has gone into our life. There are experiences and influences that come into our lives through childhood and adolescents that are instrumental in creating our dark side. The truth is, every one of us interprets what happens in life from mental pictures from experiences, and we respond to those images in the way we responded in the past, even when what we are seeing is not the same as what we have experienced. We have a tendency to predict the future from a frame of reference that was established in the past. Some dysfunction is a result of being raised in a dysfunctional environment. The Beaver System Model is helpful in understanding our families. Families are classified along five different levels of health. Level five is the family in pain. This is a seriously disturbed family. Real leadership is totally lacking and chaos, uncertainty, confusion and turmoil describe this family. There are poor boundaries; there are not clear appropriate ways of behavior because there is no sense of leadership. Maggie Scarf says, "This kind of family world is comparable to a nation in a state of civil disorder; nobody seems to have authority; nobody is able to enforce the rules or effect needed changes; real leadership is lacking." We may have come from a family where parental control was missing. We were left to figure life out for ourselves. At one point in my early childhood my father contracted polio. This was before the vaccine. He was hospitalized for a long time and my mother was left to provide for my two sisters and me, which meant working long hours as a cashier in a grocery store. It was my oldest sister's responsibility to take care of the house. This also meant watching me. Life was very chaotic and uncertain.

Level four is the borderline family. The family is polarized and instead of the chaos of the level five family, this is a dictatorship with a very rigid way of thinking, feeling and behaving expected of all members. There is no disagreement allowed. Not only are the actions to be controlled, but the thoughts and feelings of everyone are controlled also. This is an either/or environment, which means the dictator is either in control or out of control. Therefore, control is essential. You are either right or wrong, but there are no gray areas. Again, Scarf says, "An analogy might be made to the welcoming of a strong dictatorship in a country whose cultural institutions are breaking down, whose criminal justice system has ceased to function, and whose economy is out of control. In the face of total disorganization, the loss of personal freedom seems a small sacrifice; any government, however repressive, is felt to be preferable to no government at all." In this family there is no room for differences and individuality.

In level three we find a healthier environment. This is probably where the largest majority of people will find familiarity. In the mid-range family, control is not externally imposed by a dictator, but comes from the individual members of the group. There are rules, but they are often unspoken. It is the idea that "If you love me you will act in a particular way and always do things to seek my approval." Feeling loved, worthy, and good about oneself, however, depends on obeying the spoken and unspoken rules of the family. Rules are more important than the individual. A subtle level of manipulation, intimidation, and guilt fills the home. If a member of the family has an opportunity to go for a weekend with friends, and they really want to go, yet they do not want to disappoint other members of the family, they will be confronted with what is felt to be a loose/loose decision. They cannot do what they want and not disappoint the family, and if they do not do what they want they feel disappointed. Consequently, there are those rules that say, "A good husband always…." Or, "A good wife always…." "We are good children because we keep the rules." There is the ever present "invisible referee," and the sense of doing things because that is what "ought" to be done. What family members actually think and feel is sacrificed for what they *ought* to think and feel.

Level two and one are the adequate and optimal family. Here, there is the ability to be flexible and to cherish individual members and valuing a sense of closeness. Members are comfortable with feelings of annoyance and frustration with other members of the family. The difference between level two and level one is in level one the family delights in being with one another.

If we think about it, we all could say we encounter the lingering power of the family into which we were born. We leave those families when we get married, but somehow they continue to shape our lives. There are sin patterns, passed on from generation to generation in our families that are still operative in our lives. Warren Bennis said, "Given the pressures from our parents and the pressures from our peers, how does any one of us manage to emerge as sane—much less productive adults? The Waltons and the Cleavers … are far from the reality most experience. T.V. sitcom children are a good deal more likely to enjoy wise, nurturing parents and happy childhoods than the population at large." Our families were probably more in line with "Archie Bunker," "Mamma's Family" or "The Jeffersons".

Abraham Maslow theorized a hierarchy of human needs based on two groupings: deficiency needs and growth needs. Within the deficiency needs, each lower need must be met before moving to the next higher level. According to Maslow, an individual is ready to act upon the growth needs only if the deficiency needs are met. The deficiency needs are said to motivate people when they are unmet. Also, the need to fulfil such needs will become stronger the longer the duration they are denied. For example, the longer a person goes without food, the hungrier they will become.

It has been suggested that Maslow's hierarchy can be used to describe the kind of information individuals seek at different levels of development. People at the lowest level want helpful information to meet basic needs. People living on the street are looking for this kind of information. Others, at the safety level want helpful information so they can be safe and secure. If we live in a high crime area, we might be most interested in trying to make sure we are safe. We would be asking such questions as, "How can I keep from being robbed?" If we were fearful living in the same house with a father or mother, we would want to know how to protect ourselves from them.

Those at the belonging and love level are looking for enlightenment information from books and other material on relationship building. Empowerment information is sought by those at the esteem level on how to develop their ego. Because we are social beings, it is because of family, friendships and intimate connections that enables many people to get through the ups and downs of life. Lack of interactions with others, meaningful human relationships and the sense of belonging may result in depression or loneliness while an abundance of love and community often sustain people through difficult times.

The next level up the pyramid is the need for esteem. As individuals, we naturally wish to excel or be exceptional, to be noticed for our unique talents and capabilities. Once one has some measure of self-esteem and confidence, they gain the psychological freedom to be creative and to grow as well as to be more generous to others. We have a need to be valued and to have contributed to something.

Finally, those in the self-actualization level seek edifying information and seek to connect with something beyond themselves. I read that "self-actualized people tend to experience a steadier, grounded sense of well-being and satisfaction with life." According to Maslow, self-actualizing people perceive reality accurately; they have a sense of awe, wonder and gratitude about life. They are not self-centered but rather problem-centered and focus on how to improve and are not deficiency-centered. They are independent thinkers and are not overly influenced by the general culture. Their sense of humor is not sarcastic or hurtful but rather "life-affirming" with a philosophical sense of humor. They have a deeply felt sense of kinship with the human race.

The point of all this is when our basic needs are not met or we experience some traumatic event in childhood, it causes us to feel permanently threatened and we end up with missing blocks in our pyramid. We find ourselves trying to satisfy those basic needs and we are unable to develop to the level of self-actualization. This is the very heart of the dark side. These unmet needs may also aid in the development of what is labeled "existential debts;" the belief that our unmet need is our fault. Children often blame themselves for their parent's divorce. They might reason, "If I had been a good boy/girl daddy would not have left."

Allow me to touch on one more of the catalysts of the dark side. Abuse may be a real factor in dysfunctional behavior. There are several types of abuse a person may experience that could affect their ability to function appropriately. In an online article from "Child Help," it was stated that 6.6 million referrals to state protection agencies reported that 28% were for physical abuse, 20.7% sexual abuse, 10.6% emotional abuse, 9.9% physical neglect, and 14.8% emotional neglect. This doesn't even address things like sexual abuse by predators like teachers, coaches and youth leaders. Abuse may be exhibited in the form of words, actions, neglect or even spiritual abuse. What is interesting is that people who have experienced abuse, whether it is physical abuse, emotional abuse or neglect, do not perceive they have been abused. One preacher told me that his parents did not come to his installation service in his first church, and they only lived a few miles away. His wife was angry and could not understand why he wasn't angry too. To him, this neglect was normal; his parents had never come to anything he was involved in. I recently counseled a young woman who had been humiliated by her pastor. She was brought to the front of the congregation and berated in front of everyone for not tithing. Upon further questioning, it was revealed that she had been in other abusive relationships. This was normal to her. By the same token, I recall trying to help a young woman who was seeking counseling because her husband had physically assaulted her. A psychologist told me this was a healthy reaction because she had not experienced such abuse in life and recognized it as wrong.

Gregory Jantz says, "One of the most damaging effects of abuse is upon the sense of self. Any kind of abuse is an attack on a persons' sense of self." The pain that we experience in childhood has the most significance and longest lasting impact on us. Our ability to handle pain as adults is directly related to how much and what kind of pain we experienced in childhood. When we begin to look around, we see that our society, and even Christians sitting in the pews of our churches, are filled with victims of various kinds of abuse. More importantly, it also has become increasingly clear that the majority of people who are experiencing significant hindrances to success and happiness are actually victims. The result of childhood abuse may cause the minister to become pathological and invite criticism and attack due to his behavior and attitudes. Because abuse, whatever form it may take, is all about control, the minister may become neurotic and may have unusual fears or anxieties. The minister may perceives certain situations as distressing or potentially threatening to his career. One layman stated, concerning his neurotic minister, "If he can't hear the words of the Bible, 'Fear not,' then how can he expect us laymen to hear them?" Some research has suggested that our emotional responses are laid down in a broad outline in our genes, and are hard wired. This is known as our limbic system. It is here that our emotional memories are stored. It is here also that we have a trigger to make assessment of a situation automatically. If we see someone coming toward us in an aggressive manner the limbic system assesses the threat and sends a message to the neocortex where we plan a response. It is in this part of the brain that we decide we need to do something. The limbic system is an emotional filing system and it never forgets. Martha Stout in her book "The Paranoia Switch," says that trauma may actually change the functioning of our brains and it is impossible to forget the traumatic images seared into our brains. We can also develop a fear because of abuse called the "the doctrine of eligibility." It is the belief that good things happen to good people and bad things happen to bad people. It is the thinking that says, "To have something good happen in my life, I have to be good to be eligible for it." The same is true about if we are bad, then bad things might happen to us. One of the most prevalent results of abuse is low self-esteem. This results in a person habitually giving in to the desires of others because of distrust of their own ability and competency. This will also mean a general lack of self-confidence and will be demonstrated by a difficulty in making decisions. Everyone needs to feel special and appreciated, but if you have experienced abuse in any of its ugly forms, that feeling of being special and appreciated has been absent. Consequently, to fill that need you may substitute something else. This is known as transfer of needs and is exhibited in all types of addiction, including workaholics. The minister may have a histrionic personality disorder where he is overly emotional and attention seeking. The DSM-IV says, "A man with this disorder may dress and behave in a manner often identified as 'macho' and may seek to center attention by bragging about athletic skills, whereas a woman, for example, may choose very feminine clothes and talk about how much she impressed her dance instructor." A very interesting effect of abuse is what is known as "failure syndrome." The abused person does not feel he is good enough to win so subconsciously sabotages his own career by entering into conduct he knows will be to his destruction. Perfectionism is another result of abuse. The perfectionism may not be just directed inward, but it may also be directed outward, causing the minister to have the same expectations from others as he has from himself. There is also what as been called, "The Bully" minister. These pastors are deeply insecure and need to control others for fear their world will come crashing in on them if they are not in control. Because they may have been abused they now subconsciously may be seeking to get even with their abuser in a symbolic substitutionary way.

The minister may also have a crisis orientation. The abused person thrives on being the person that fixes things. If a crisis does not happen frequently enough so he can rush in and save the day, he may create a crisis or turn everyday problems into crisis'. The minister who uses anger in unhealthy, excessive ways may invite criticism and attack. Perhaps he learned in childhood that the best way to deal with a problem or with problem people was the use of anger. If a minister wants his people to be angry and critical, then all he has to do is be angry and show a judgmental attitude.

If you have experienced abuse in the past there are emotional tests, and if you suspect some pathological behavior, you should seek professional help from a trained counselor. There are several psychological tests available from therapists to help assist the therapist in diagnosis. Such as: The Minnesota Multiphasic Personality Inventory and the Basic Personality Inventory. There is no shame in needing help. The shame comes from not seeking help when it is needed. This does not mean you are crazy, but it does mean you need some help to overcome.

When we start to see all of the things that go into the dark side, it is amazing that any of us can function. Again, we have to realize that everyone since Adam and Eve is dysfunctional, because we are not what we were designed to be. Our bodies and minds have been corrupted by sin. Most people suffer to some degree, great or small, from at least one of the problems we have discussed. However, recognizing a personal dysfunction enables us to mitigate its effects. It is not a matter of whether or not we have a particular dysfunction, but a matter of being able to keep it from affecting our ability to relate to others without that dysfunction sabotaging the relationship. I have included a self-test in the appendix to help you discover where you are dysfunctional. When you discover your personal dysfunction you will need to determine how debilitating it has been on your ministry, and what you will need to do next. There may be some things you recognize and can determine how to minimize their impact on your relationships. You may determine these issues have caused a great deal of trouble, and you need someone to help you get some control. In that case, you will want to contact a professional counselor. As a child of God, you deserve the best help available, and your ministry is too important to worry about having all the answers, and being the person who everyone else comes to when they need help. You are not Superman or Superwoman. I want to reiterate that this is not all bad news. There are some aspects to the dark side that help make people successful. Those very same dysfunctions that hurt the people I have mentioned were dysfunctions that drove them to success. Would they have been successful had they not been dysfunctional? Yes, but without the relational problems they encountered because of their dysfunction.

Because of our families and experiences there is plenty of room to place the blame for our dysfunction on things external to ourselves. We live in a victim oriented society, that seeks to blame all of its bad behavior on someone or something, rather than assuming responsibility. This is not designed to allow you to do that with your personal dysfunction. We all have had things stack up against us that were bigger than what we could overcome. We may very well have come from a level five family, where chaos reigned. We may not have had our basic needs met as a child, but our problems are now ours to deal with.

There was a boy born in Oklahoma who by the time he was 12 his family had moved 14 times. His father was an abusive alcoholic. When he was old enough, he left home and joined the military. While stationed in Korea he became fascinated with Marshall Arts. He was a national champion several times. You may be familiar with him. His name is Chuck Norris, and his story is in the book "Against All Odds." The point here is that we may have come from dysfunctional families, but our families do not determine our destinies. Your family does not define who you are. Only God, as your Creator, has the right to define you. He says you have been redeemed, and you are a new creation. We can say with the Apostle Paul, "We are more than conquerors through Christ."

The survival tip of being aware of our closest enemy is not exciting, but as you take the test and learn about your personal dysfunction, it will enable you to take steps to reduce the impact that dysfunction has upon your ministry.

Appendix A is a test adapted from "The Dark Side of Leadership," using questions designed specifically for ministers. I would like to especially call your attention to the bibliography at the end of the chapter. For further study I would recommend "The Dark Side of Leadership," Leading with a Limp," and "The Emotionally Healthy Church."

Allender, D. (2006). "Leading With A Limp". Colorado Springs, Co. Waterbrook Press

Bennis, W. (1989). *On Becoming a Leader* Reading, NY. Addison-Wesley

Blotnik, S. (1987). "Ambitious Men: Their Drive, Dreams and Delusions" New York, NY. Viking Penguin Inc.

Burns, J. *Leadership* (New York: 1978),78; quoted in Gary L. McIntosh and Samuel Rima, *Overcoming the Dark Side of Leadership* (Grand Rapids: Baker Books, 1997), 56.

Buhler, R. (1991) *Pain and Pretending* Nashville,Tenn. Thomas Nelson

Canfield, J. (2005). "The Success Principles" New York, NY. HarperCollins Pub.

Diagnostic and Statistical Manual of Mental Disorders, 4th ed. (Washington, D.C.: American Psychiatric Association, 1994), 656.

Eckman, P. (2003). *Emotions Revealed*. New Your, N.Y. Owl Books

Goleman, D. (2006). "Social Intelligence",New York, NY. Bantam Books

Greenfield,G. (2005). *The Wounded Minister*.Grand Rapids, Mich. Baker Books

Huitt,W. "Maslow's Hierarchy Of Needs," *Educational Psychology Interactive*, 2007, www.edpsycinteractive.org/topic/regsys/maslow.html. (accessed March 1, 2010).

Jantz, G.(2009). *Healing the Scars of Emotional Abuse* (Grand Rapids, Mich. Revell

Living Waters Ministry, November 14, 2008, "Codependency," http://blog.livingwatersministry.com/ (accessed December 6).

Martin, R. (1995). "Seeds of Destruction: Joe Kennedy and His Sons" New York, NY. G.P. Putnam's Sons

McIntosh, G. and Rima, S. (1997). *Overcoming the Dark Side of Leadership* Grand Rapids, Mich. Baker Books

McNeal, R. (2003). The Present Future. San Francisco, CA. Jossey Bass Pub.

Norris, C. (2004). "Against All Odds" Nashville, Tenn. B&H Publishers

Oswald, R. (1993). *Finding Leaders for Tomorrow's Churches* (Washington , D.C.: The Alban Institute, 1993); quoted in Norman Shawchuck and Roger Heuser, *Managing the Congregation* (Nashville: Abingdon Press, 1996),

Parson, G. and Leas,S.(1993). *Understanding Your Congregation As a System* (Herndon: The Alban Institute

Scarf, M. (1995). *Intimate Worlds: Life Inside the Family*. New York, NY. Random House

Scazzero, P. (2003). *The Emotionally Healthy Church* .Grand Rapids, Mich. Zondervan

Stout, M. *The Paranoia Switch* New York, NY Sarah Crichton

Thornton, J. "The Limbic System And Your Emotions," www.the biggestideas.com/ (accessed June 13,2010).

SURVIVAL TIP #5
Work on the Inside First

My second car was a 1956, Volkswagon Beetle, with a ragtop sunroof. I had it painted a deep navy blue because I was in the Navy at the time. I cut the rear wheel wells out and got chrome reverse wheels and wide tires. I wanted it to look cool. As a matter of fact, I was far more concerned about how it looked than how it ran. I recently bought a new pickup truck. My old truck was18 years old with 170,000 miles on it. It had some pretty good dents in it and the seats were torn, but I had just had a new heater core and air conditioning evaporator installed. The mechanic went over the drive train, front to rear, and it ran like a top. The difference in the two vehicles is, I realized that what was most important was what was on the inside and not what was on the outside.

From what we saw in the last chapter, it is obvious that the things that cause us the greatest frustration, disappointment and difficulty is working with the people we are trying to lead. I looked back at my ministry and thought about how knowing some relational skills could have made a great difference in my ministry. There were things I could have done that would have had a greater impact than all of the programs I tried.

College taught me all about theology, eschatology, soteriology and a dozen other "ologies" in school. They taught me how to put a sermon together with three points, and an introduction, and a conclusion that grabs people. I learned about church administration, serving communion, doing funerals and weddings. I trudged through subjects like "Western Civilization," and loved "Psalms." In graduate school I learned about hermeneutics, and more theology. I am grateful for all I learned, and for the men and women who invested their lives in me. Some had to endure my sleepy attendance in class, others answering questions after class. But, sadly, nothing was taught about relationships. In ministry, I was going to work with people, not books or machines. People needed more than what was in my brain; they needed me. It was not enough that I had baggage of which I was not even aware, but I lacked skills in developing close relationships with the people I was going to lead.

I needed to learn relational skills. Consequently, I devoured Daniel Goleman's books, "Emotional Intelligence," and the sequel to that, "Social Intelligence." From there it was a natural jump to his book, "Primal Leadership," and Malcom Gladwell's book, "The Tipping Point," and Travis Bradberry's "Emotional Intelligence 2.0". I want to share with you one of the most important tips for pastoral survival in how to effectively relate to people.

The Christian faith is unarguably about relationship. That relationship is both vertical with God, and horizontal with people. I heard a sermon series that was entitled, "Good with God, But Not with People." We don't have a problem with our relationship with God, but we do struggle in our relationships with people. As the old poem said, "Oh to be with angels above, that will be glory. To be with people below is another story." I have said, "Pastoring would be great if it wasn't for people." Our problems are not with the world and outside influences nearly as much as it is with the people we are trying to lead. Working with things is no problem at all. Working with people can be exasperating, frustrating, and down right infuriating at times. If we don't know what causes our relational problem's we will keep doing the same aggravating and irritating things. Having pastored in Louisiana, I am reminded of the story of when Boudreaux explained to Thibodeaux the "deeference between de words aggravation and irreetation." Boudreaux said, "pass me dat talafoam book dere. Ahm gon' sho ys da deeference rat now." Boudreaux selected a number at random from de book, dialed eet and a woman answered. "Hallo," said Boudreaux. "Ahd like ta talk weet Boudreaux." De woman replied sweetly, "Ahm sorry, sir, mais you have de wrong number." Boudreaux apologized and hung up.

He waited a minute, den he redialed de woman's number. When de woman answered, he said, "Kin ah talk weet Boudreaux please?" "You must be the same gentleman who called before," she said. "Ahm sorry, mais you've dialed the wrong number again." He apologized once more. A minute later he dialed the same number and said, "Uuuh, lemme talk wit Boudreaux." By now, de woman wuz obviously angry. "Look, I've tole you twice dat dere's no Boudreaux living here! Don't budder me again!" Wit dat, she slammed de phone down. Boudreaux turned to Thibodeaux and said, "Now, you see dere, Thibodeaux, dat's irreetation. Na ahm goin' sho yaw at aggravation is." Boudreaux dialed de number again. When de woman answered, he said, "Oh beb, did is Boudreaux, anybody call for me?" When we have relational problems we go from irritation to aggravation.

I suppose all of that is humorous, but the fact and reality of the need to have good relational skills is not a joke. We can look around and see how the people who are most successful in ministry are the same people with good relational skills. We might think they are gifted in that area or its their temperament, and to some extent that may be true, but again, that is not an excuse for us to be relationally challenged. That is just a politically correct way of saying, we have trouble with maintaining and building real relationships with the people we lead. We can make excuses and blame our families, our education, the places we minister, but excuses are just exits to succeeding, and as John Maxwell said, "When you blame, you "Be-lame." Wayne Dyer, in the book, "How to Get What You Really, Really, Really, Really Want," said, "All blame is a waste of time. No matter how much fault you find with another, and regardless of how much you blame him, it will not change you." George Washington Carver said, "Ninety-nine percent of all failures come from people who have a habit of making excuses." When we accepted the call to minister, just like the first disciples, we accepted the call to learn. You didn't know how to preach until you were taught, and if you are not a good preacher you should be trying to be a better preacher. If we aren't good with our interpersonal skills, we should be trying to get better. Even if we are good at those things we should be trying to improve. The past is the past. All that matters now, is what happens from this point forward. And before you begin to think that what is known as emotional intelligence is not necessary, or something trendy, realize that there have been more than 3,000 studies to show its value. In an article from "Inc.," Justin Bariso writes about "How a Lack of Emotional Intelligence Kills Your Personal Brand." I realize this is from the business world, but as he points out, "perception is reality," to people in the world. It is the same in the church. I was stunned as I read what he goes on to say. He had been reading my book. No, that's not possible because it had not been published yet. But there it was. As I said in chapter 1, "People will forget what you said, people will forget what you did, but people will never forget how you made them feel." How we make people feel will determine in great part how they will perceive our ministry, our brand, our Christianity. You have said it: "The only Jesus people will see is the Jesus in you and me." Emotional intelligence is realized in the power of the Holy Spirit, using skills that demonstrate self-control and empathy. Malcom Gladwell wrote the great little book, "The Tipping Point: How Little Things Can Make a Big Difference." The point of the book and the point concerning emotional intelligence is that being emotionally intelligent is not a big ostentatious thing, but a change in ourselves that may not be perceived by others until they have been around us for awhile. Then they will say, "What has changed about you? There is something different about how you react and treat people."

In 1974 Morris Albert wrote a song, the title of which is "Feelings." His song was about his feelings of a lost love, and how those feelings were overwhelming him. This chapter isn't about the feelings of a lost love, but it is about having our feelings under control. There actually is a science that studies feelings and how people relate and what are some of the things that make one person better at certain relationship skills than another. Why do some people make us feel comfortable, while others make us feel uneasy? Why do some people handle stress better than others? These are questions that are investigated under the science of neuroscience, which is the study of the brain. While I have read some about this I must confess I do not understand much of it at all. We don't need to understand the science of how the brain works to benefit from understanding some of what it does. We all know that the brain is the command center for all we do. Everything comes through our senses and is processed in the brain. Then the brain sends out commands and action is taken. There has been a great deal of study in genetics that seems to point to relational abilities being partly in our genes. One scientist, Jerome Kagan, a Harvard psychologist says that a trait of temperament like inhibition had biological causes. Neuroscience is discovering a list of behavioral habits that are controlled by a portion of our DNA. The theory then is the way we relate to others is genetic; a biological condition. It has to do with the "way we are wired." Certainly, we could agree that some seem to be more predisposed relationally than others.

There is also the explanation that we are a product of our environment. We function socially because of the way we were raised. If we came from a well adjusted, caring, loving family we are better at relating to people than if we came from an abusive environment with alcoholic parents. We may be more socially competent because we have seen relationships lived out. Childhood and adolescence are important times for establishing emotional habits that will govern our lives. As was chronicled in the previous chapter, we are products of our families and experiences. But our destiny is not in our genes or in our past.

We have looked at two things that we might not know that can hurt us. The third thing we have not learned is, good, effective relational skills. We have all worked for and with people we struggled with in productively relating to them. I worked in one of those home improvement stores for a while, thinking it would be great to help people find that thing they were looking for to complete a project at home. One of the managers treated everyone with an attitude of a Marine drill sergeant, which meant they was little or no social skills and you simply wanted to avoid contact with them. If you saw that manager, you went the other way. The call from this manager over the personal announcement system sounded like that drill sergeant calling for ten more push ups. Needless to say, when that manager wasn't on duty I was glad. I am sure this has brought to mind people with whom you have associated. But, think about those people in your life you have liked working for and with. Think about those people who have had the most positive influence on you. Recall the best boss you ever worked for. Who have been the people who have inspired you to do and be your best? Why did you like them, work hard for them and perhaps even revere them? There also was another manager who used emotional and social intelligence skills, whether he realized it or not, when interacting with the employees. This man was an encourager and a pleasure to work for and work with. He demonstrated a genuine interest in those he worked with. I was always glad to see him coming. There was no task that wasn't a pleasure to undertake in which I wanted to do my very best. Today, if that man called me and asked for help I would gladly go help him without any hesitation. What was the difference? Emotional intelligence. There was a difference in the way he saw me that made me feel like I mattered. We can become competent and emotionally intelligent leaders. At the end of this chapter I have listed some very good resources you can use and learn more about these skills. These skills will take some very intentionality and time, as well as practice, but it is not just a matter of skills learned. The skills are important, but it also involves a different mindset. I will get to that in awhile, but I want to make you aware of the main components of emotional intelligence, and from there it will be up to you. And before we go any further, let me say that while many of the things that I am postulating come from the business world they are found in biblical principles.

There are four areas that need our attention. Two of them are personal intelligence skills; self-awareness, self-management, and two are social intelligent skills; social awareness, and relationship management. As we look at these four areas, it should be noted that it begins with self-awareness and self-management. You and I know this as the fruit of the Spirit of self-control. If any people can master relationship skills it should be the people of God, and most certainly, the people God has called to lead His people. Preaching is a skill that can be learned, and there are skills in leadership. There are also skills we can learn on relating better. These skills will need to be bathed in prayer and empowered by the Spirit. All of this has to do with our emotions.

We need to see that emotions are God-given. They are not evil. Adam had emotions before the fall. God is portrayed as having emotions. Jesus displayed emotions. Emotions are not sinful in and of themselves. They are quite wonderful, and even helpful when they do not run amuck. The Bible is filled with verses about our emotions.

Psalm 139:13 says, "For you created my inmost being; you knit me together in my mothers' womb." The words, "inmost being" is kidneys. It was believed that the kidneys were the place of sorrow and rejoicing. When I was a boy, we would call my grandmother on special occasions. As soon as she knew it was us she would begin to cry. My dad said, "Her kidneys were behind her eyeballs." There may be something to that. We are emotional creatures. We feel sad, happy, frightened, anxious, nervous, depressed, excited, bored and many other emotions. We experience emotions everyday many, many times a day. Part of the problem involves not being aware of those emotions as we experience them, and we are even able to name the emotion. We feel something, but we are not able to say to ourselves, "Right now, I am feeling...." Emotions are "in essence, impulses to act, the instant plans for handling life that evolution has instilled in us. The very root of the word emotion is *motere*, the Latin verb "to move," plus the prefix "e-" to connote "move away," suggesting that a tendency to act is implicit in every emotion." If we do not act outwardly, we act inwardly. You have heard someone say, "That really ate at me." Or, "That tore me up inside." When you preach you are not primarily appealing to the intellect of the people. You are appealing to their emotions. Why? Because it is our emotions that move us to act. You communicate your message as much through your emotions as you do your words; actually, even more so. You wouldn't think of just reading your message to people. You communicate emotion through your tone and volume, your facial expressions, and gestures. Let me repeat this: we are emotional creatures. Now you can have a frontal lobotomy, which will make you very nearly totally unemotional. This was a procedure done many years ago on the criminally insane to keep them from being out of control. In the 1975 movie, "One Flew Over the Cuckoo's Nest," starring Jack Nicholson, the movie ends with that procedure having been performed on him. He went from a man institutionalized, who wasn't really insane, to being made a veritable vegetable. Since that is not likely to happen to you or me, we need to learn to deal with emotions. Daniel Goleman writes in "Primal Leadership," "The fundamental task of leaders, we argue, is to prime good feeling in those they lead…. At its root, then, the primal job of leadership is emotional." We become all we can be when we are around people who make us feel good about who we are and what we are doing. That does not mean we are on the "Good Ship Lollipop" and we don't confront sin or people when they are acting inappropriately. It does mean that if you want people to respond positively to your ministry you will need to relate to them in a way that makes them want to respond positively. I think this is more true in the church than anywhere else. We are dealing with a volunteer workforce. They are not worried about a paycheck or being fired. If they do not want to follow your leadership you cannot reprimand them or fire them.

Much stock is placed in IQ, intellect quotient. This measures how smart we are. EQ is emotional intelligence. The fact is, that the people with high EQ will be more successful than the people with only high IQ. As a university instructor, I have students who can do great work and make 'A's' on all their papers, but they are socially and emotionally immature. They do well academically, but unless they learn emotionally intelligent skills they will be failures in ministry. If we rely on IQ it is like a bird trying to fly with one wing. IQ deals with the head and EQ deals with the heart. When we put IQ with EQ we have feeling and thought. Your EQ is the thing that impacts most everything you say and do. EQ is so critical to your success that it accounts for almost 60 percent of performance in all types of jobs. Some believe that EQ is the single biggest predictor of performance and the strongest driver of leadership and personal excellence.

Here is the good news. Our IQ is our ability to learn and it is fixed. Whatever our IQ is at 12, it will be the same when we are 60. EQ, on the other hand, can increase with learning and practice. You may have very little EQ, but you can learn and practice the skills and increase your EQ.

I already mentioned the four areas of EQ, and the first is being self-aware. We cannot lead others until we can lead ourselves, and we cannot lead ourselves until we know ourselves. I realize that this sounds like we are revisiting the previous chapter, but we are not. Travis Bradberry writes, "Only 36 percent of the people we tested are able to accurately identify their emotions as they happen." We are experiencing emotions all the time, but we are not conscious enough to even be able to label the emotions as they happen. This means that two thirds of people are typically controlled by their emotions and are not yet skilled at spotting them and using them to their benefit. The reality is that 83 percent of the people considered to be the top performers in their field are people who are self-aware. Emotional awareness and understanding are not taught in school. We enter the ministry knowing how to do all the things that require knowledge, but too often, we lack the skills to manage our emotions in the heat of the challenging problems that we face. Good decisions require far more than factual knowledge. Good decisions are made using self-knowledge and emotional mastery when they're needed most. This is the foundation of emotional intelligence.

There are actually two sides to the mind. We have a rational side that controls the mind where we can think about things that happen to us. There is the emotional mind, which reacts to what happens to us. There is that part of the brain that deals with the "fight or flight" response. Some believe that God created us like that because our very early ancestor's needed to react quickly. The difference of reacting immediately and thinking about it could mean being the main course of some predatory animal or being killed by an adversary. One night, in the middle of the night, our security system began to blare with that loud warning scream. It was saying, 'Someone is in the house!' I jumped out of bed, ran down the hall to the living room to find nothing. I turned off the alarm and headed back to bed. It occurred to me that there could have been an armed assailant that I would have come face to face with. All of a sudden, I got chills and became nauseous thinking about the possibilities. When I jumped out of bed I was acting from my emotions and not from the rational, thinking part of my brain. The part of the brain that triggers emotional response is called the amygdala, and it is located at the base of the brain. The rational part of the brain that controls our emotional reactions is the prefrontal cortex, which is located in the front of the brain. The problem is something happens and before the prefrontal cortex can analyze and control what we do with the emotion, we have already acted. I saw a cartoon that said, "Y'know, most aggression is carried out in the heat of the moment…we have waiting periods with guns—if only we could have the same thing with emotions."

While interpersonal intelligence means understanding other people, being self-aware means having intrapersonal intelligence, which is to have a truthful and accurate idea of yourself and being able to use that to effectively live. There are real scientific ways of describing what it is to be self-aware, but it is experiencing an emotion yet, not being controlled by it. It is to be able to understand you are experiencing an emotion and be able to say, "I am experiencing…." and begin to think of ways to properly respond to that emotion. As the Greek philosopher Epictetus wrote, "It's not what happens to you, but how you react to it that matters." Too often, we react before we can analyze and respond in a more appropriate and productive manner. As one writer terms it, "in unresourceful ways." As Travis Bradberry says, "Emotional intelligence is your ability to recognize and understand emotions in yourself and others, and your ability to use this awareness to manage your behavior and relationships."

One of the problems of being self-aware is our eyes are fixed in the front of our heads, which means, unless we are looking in a mirror or watching ourselves in a video, we normally don't see ourselves. Self-awareness during conflict includes not only being able to see yourself, but to be able to perceive how the other people involved in the conflict see you. Other people see your body language and tone of voice and interpret these signals through their own perceptual filters. To understand how another person is feeling, you need to get a sense of how they are seeing you. Too often, we are not aware of our tone of voice or facial expressions. These things counter our words. People hear what we are saying, but they also hear our tone and see what our faces say. Being self-aware mean being able to see yourself as others see you. What is it like interacting with you? How do you come across with the people you work with?

Unfortunately, we have each seen too many times what happens when our emotions get triggered during conflict. Your reactions may include anger, defensiveness, blaming, attacking, stonewalling, yelling, clamming up or shutting down, in varying degrees or combinations; our reactions are as individual as we are. Any of these or other unproductive reactions can throw a monkey wrench into what might otherwise have been productive conflict-resolution. So what triggers these reactions in you? Only you can answer that question. If you can identify and monitor your triggers during a conflict, you have a much better chance of keeping the triggers from being unconsciously pulled. Being self-aware means what I would call being continually mindful. It's about being aware of each moment and everything around you. By practicing mindfulness on a daily basis you'll naturally become more self-aware and better able to manage your emotions and difficult relationships.

People high in self-awareness are also remarkably clear in their understanding of what they do well, what motivates and satisfies them, and which people and situations push their buttons. Self-aware people are aware of their values; what is most important to them, and they are able to act accordingly. Being self-aware also means being aware of our abilities and talents and gifts, as well as our dysfunctions.

The second part of emotional intelligence is self-management. Scripturally, that is known as self-control. Emotional intelligence is found all through the book of Proverbs and the Wisdom literature. We want to be people controlled by the Holy Spirit, but the truth of the matter is we often fail to control or manage our emotions. Sometimes they spill out all over people. I recall an incident where I called my wife to tell her I was coming home, as I had been doing something beyond my normal time for coming home. I called and got her voice mail. I called again, and again got her voice mail. I realized that she probably was on the phone with someone and she doesn't like taking another call. I called a third time with the same results. Now, I am getting irritated. What if I was in an emergency?

By the fourth call I had moved beyond irritated to aggravated (remember the difference?). I walked in the door to find my wife on the phone, as I expected. I scowled at her and said, in a rather angry tone, "When I call you would you please answer the phone?" Can I tell you it did not go well from there? I thought, I should have handled that differently. I should have waited until I was not angry and made a request giving reasons why it was important for her to take my call. On another occasion, we were driving down the road and my wife was on the phone with my daughter. I overheard her say, "Sure, dad will pick her up." She was volunteering me to pick my granddaughter up at school. Now, I love my granddaughter, and I don't mind picking her up, but I was not even asked if I would mind doing so. I was seriously annoyed at what seemed to me to be a lack of consideration. I was aware of my feelings and determined that my response in that moment might not be productive. I decided to give some thought to a productive way to handle this problem. Thirty minutes later, after considering my words, I confronted my wife in a way that did not put her on the defensive and she was apologetic. What a difference being self-awareness made in the two scenarios. Do I now do that all the time, since I have learned to be self-aware? No, but I am getting better. I have seen what a difference it can make in relating with my wife.

The fact is, we cannot choose our emotions. The idea is not to get rid of emotions, but to find a balance between intellect and emotions and harmonize the heart with the head. But, we must manage them for they are contagious. Hamlet said, "Give me a man that is not passion's slave...." A sense of self-mastery, of being able to withstand the emotional storms is what the Bible calls temperance. We have to understand that our emotions are contagious. Smile at someone and watch them smile back. Just as a yawn is contagious so are our emotions. Whenever we detect excitement in someone's voice, see anger in their eyes, or discouragement in their posture we react to that. This is called the open-loop where how other people can change our emotions. There is even a physiological change that occurs in us. In Daniel Goleman's book "Social Intelligence," he says we have neural Wi Fi. When we see an emotion expressed on someone's face, there are "mirror" neurons in the brain that reflect back the action we see. I think we need to understand that self-management doesn't mean just managing negative emotions, but also positive emotions. If we want the people of our congregation to experience positive emotions, then we must display positive emotions. This contagion comes from the top down, and not from the bottom up. People catch what the leader has. Leaders can give praise or withhold it, criticize constructively or destructively, offer support or be blind to people's needs. They can give meaning to everyone's contribution, or not. They can guide in such a way as to give a sense of direction or they can allow people to flounder. They can encourage flexibility, and by doing so set people free to use their talents, abilities and knowledge to do a good job, or they can micro-manage. This is all a matter of emotional acumen. Being self-aware means being aware of an emotion we are experiencing and our thoughts about that emotion. It is being aware of an emotion and being able to look at it objectively, and even realizing the need to adjust how you need to react. After all, as I stated earlier, the root meaning of the word emotion means "to move." Emotions are impulses to move or to do something like fight or flight. As Goleman writes, "There is perhaps no psychological skill more fundamental than resisting impulse. It is the root of all emotional self-control, since the emotions, by their very nature, lead to one or another impulse to act." This is not just about reacting to what people do and say, but about realizing any impulse to act. It also means being able to delay gratification.

Perhaps you have heard of the experiment with young children on delayed gratification. They gave a group of children each a cookie and told them they could eat the cookie if they wanted or, if they would wait until the adult came back in the room they could have two cookies. If they didn't wait, they only got the one cookie. Some children went to great lengths to wait, singing and playing, while others couldn't wait and ate the cookie. Those same children were followed through high school. It was discovered that the children who were able to delay gratification were far more successful than those who were unable to do so. Unfortunately, we live in a society that scorns delayed gratification. We want it all and we want it now. A recent report revealed that 36% of Americans are living paycheck-to-paycheck and 19% are even worse off than that. That is to say, many are living beyond their financial means. Delayed gratification isn't limited to our spending habits. It also means being willing to take the time necessary to make change in our congregations. Too often, we want that change to happen now, and when change doesn't take place fast enough we move on, or we try to force change. Remember, only two people like change; babies with their diapers, and leaders, if it is their idea.

Being self-aware means being able to better manage stress because you know that stress is caused by your own perception of a situation. We know that we usually perceive things as being blown out of proportion to what they really are, and when we make decisions they are too often wrong decisions. I recall one year-end performance evaluation I had on a job, and began to imagine how the supervisor was going to make sure they didn't make me feel too good so there would be no need to think about a raise. I was nervous and even began to get angry. As I became aware of my emotions I realized I was getting upset when I didn't even know what the evaluation would be. I was able to change my thinking, change my emotions and when it came time for the evaluation I was confident and ready. They fired me. No, not really. The evaluation was better than I could have hoped for. If we are self-aware we can assess the positives and negatives of a situation and resolve it. It won't be a resolution based on emotion.

I think about doing conferences with what I have written and I know the worst people for a preacher to speak to is other preachers. I get butterflies and my heart rate goes up. I begin to sweat and my mouth gets dry. I am seeing it from my perspective. But if I begin to think about seeing it from outside of me, I see people who want to be able to minister more effectively. Pastors are always looking for something that will help them be a better pastor. They are hopeful and expecting people. They know what it is like to bring truth to people with the desire that they will receive it. Wow! This is great. What better opportunity to minister to people than to people who want to be ministered unto? My nervousness moves from anxiety and stress to excitement and positive anticipation. The result of my self-awareness is it makes those I'm addressing positive because my emotion is contagious.

Because of not just being self-aware, but also managing self, the emotional intelligent person lives out their values. The person who does not manage themselves does not act in accord with what they say their values are. They are the person who says, "My health is important," but does not exercise or eat healthy, or the individual who says, "My family is most important," but spends more time at work, or pursuing hobbies or sports, than with family. Self aware people do not act in opposition to their core values. Survival tip #5 is a life changer and a leadership changer.

I have provided a mini test on emotional intelligence in the Appendix B. However, if you purchase Travis Bradberry's book, "Emotional Intelligence 2.0," a free online emotional intelligence test is given. You will want to refer to this resource, as it is one of the best.

Bradberry, T. (2009). Emotional Intelligence 2.0. San Diego, Cal. Talent Smart

Goleman, D. (1995). Emotional Intelligence. New York, NY. Bantam Dell

Goleman, D. (2006). Social Intelligence. New York, NY. Bantam Dell

SURVIVAL TIP #6
Be Aware of Others

Having looked at the intrapersonal skills of being self-aware and self-managing, let's turn our attention to the third and fourth areas of emotional intelligence which, involves interpersonal relation skills. If we are to be effective leaders, we need social awareness. Social awareness is your ability to accurately perceive and recognize the emotions in other people. It also means understanding what is really going on with them. This often means discerning what other people are thinking and feeling, even if you do not feel the same way. The failure to recognize the feelings of others is a major shortcoming in having rapport with people. Rapport comes from the ability to be attuned to others and to have empathy. It's is so easy to get caught up in our own emotions and forget to consider the perspective of other people. Social awareness endeavors to stay focused and gain critical information. Listening and observing are the most important elements of social awareness. The Bible says, "Weep with those who weep and rejoice with those who rejoice." To listen well and observe what's going on around us, we have to stop doing many things we like to do. We have to stop talking, stop figuring out what we are going to say next. This means being fully present. Whenever our attention is divided, we tune out just a little bit, and when we do so we miss important emotional details.

I mentioned mirror neurons in the previous chapter, and social skills depend on these neurons. When we mimic what another person does or feels, these neurons create a shared sensibility. As Goleman says, "To understand another, we become like the other—at least a bit." Someone tells you about something that is troubling them and as you listen your face begins to resemble the same sadness that is evident on their face. If we are to pick up on the emotional cues that people give, we must be totally present. In the book "5 Gears," the introduction starts by describing a very familiar scenario. "You're here, but you're really not here. You are with me, but you're somewhere far away." Your wife says, "You haven't heard a word I was saying." You heard, but really didn't hear. Why? Well, I confess I am a little hard of hearing from having worked on jet engines for years. However, most of the time we don't hear is because we are not present. When we can have the ability to connect with others and be present, we will be able to build long-term relationships. Multi-tasking is a killer here. Think of a time when you were trying to share something with someone and they were looking around or texting. You were trying to connect with them. You were trying to tell them something you thought was important, and they were sending you the signal that this is not important to them. I remember when I first learned about being present, I thought about times when I haven't been present. When I was busy with something I was really interested in, or when there was a football game on. Sometimes, we aren't present when someone is telling us something we are not interested in. Before I had grandchildren I wondered what the big deal was when people wanted to show me pictures of their precious little grandchild. Too often, I had the attitude that said, "Big deal. I am not really interested in your grandchildren." There have been those times when I have been looking for something on the internet like another book I just had to have. My wife has tried to tell me something and I would give the perfunctory, uh huh! Only later to find she was trying to tell me something important and I didn't really hear. Too often, we judge what is important by whether or not it is important to us, rather than if it is important to the other person. What our children think is exciting, troubling, interesting or important very likely will not evoke that same emotion in us. How present are we to them when they share those things? People we minister to are the same way. They want to share things that are exciting, troubling, interesting and important to them, and when we do not give them the attention that they think is warranted, we are failing in interpersonal relationships.

People's emotions are seldom put into words. Real listening requires that we be attuned to their feelings. Emotions are usually expressed through facial cues; our eyes or body language say more than our words. Actually, our eyes and body language may contradict our words. The key to being able to discern people's feelings is being able to read their facial expressions, the tone of their voice or gestures. Ninety percent or more of an emotional message is nonverbal, and if we are not attuned to people we will miss those messages. Even when we are not talking we continue to send signals about what we feel with our expressions.

The dictionary defines empathy as "the feeling that you understand and share another person's experiences and emotions." When we are able to empathize with people we leave them feeling understood and cared for. If we go back to the first chapter of this book, I said that we need to love the people we are serving. If we are to love them, we must empathize with them. The word empathy comes from a German word that literally translates as "feeling into," suggesting an inner imitation of the other person's feelings. When we connect with people at an emotional level it makes work more meaningful. Goleman says, "When leaders are able to grasp other people's feelings and perspectives, they access a potent emotional guidance system that keeps what they say and do on track." Now I know this is not rocket science, but when we keep the emotions and perspectives of others in mind we will shape what we say and do in ways that are productive. I was having some questions about our finances at home and needed to talk to my wife about it. One of the three things that causes divorce is money, and I am sure you probably have had some heated discussions about money with your spouse. I was seeking to be sensitive to my wife's feelings that enabled me to talk about the finances in a way that did not place her on the defensive. Empathic listening has been said to be one of the top three abilities of people rated as being outstanding in their organizations. They don't just listen to the things people say, they attune to their emotions. Then they go beyond that and ask questions to better understand.

Daniel Goleman relays a story that perfectly illustrates the idea of being attuned to another's feelings. He writes, "Shortly after Takeo Doi, a Japanese psychiatrist, arrived on his first visit to America, he had an awkward moment. He was visiting the home of someone to whom he had just been introduced, and his host asked Doi if he was hungry, adding, 'We have some ice cream if you'd like.'

Doi was in fact hungry. But being asked point-blank if he was hungry by someone he hardly knew was jarring. He would never have been asked such a thing in Japan.

Following the norms of Japanese culture, Doi could not bring himself to admit hunger. So he passed up the offer of the ice cream.

At the same time Doi recalls cherishing a mild hope that his host would press him again. He was disappointed to hear his host say, 'I see,' and dropped the offer.

In Japan, Doi notes, a host would simply have sensed his hunger and given him something to eat without having to ask if he wanted it.

This does not mean you need to be cognizant of cultural norms from other countries, but had the host been attuned to Doi he may have just brought him some ice cream. That sensing of another person's needs and feelings, and the unsolicited response to them, bespeaks the high value on the [empathic] mode in Japanese culture (and in East Asian cultures generally). The Japanese word *amae* refers to this sensibility, empathy that is taken for granted, and acted upon, without calling attention to itself.

In the orbit of *amae* we feel felt. Takeo Doi sees the warm connectedness of the mother-infant relationship— in which the mother intuitively senses what the baby needs—as the prototype of this heightened attunement. It extends into every close social tie in Japanese daily life, creating an intimate atmosphere of connectedness."

This is a social skill found in waiters of really good restaurants. The normal, very irritating scenario in a restaurant is you are either forever trying to find the person responsible for the care of those at the table, or they come by the table every five minutes and ask you if you need anything and asking if everything is okay. A good waiter anticipates the needs and watches the table. They notice your glass of tea is low and come and fill it. There are no dinner rolls left, so they go get some more. They are attuned to our needs and that is appreciated without being bothersome.

We cannot manage ourselves until we know ourselves. We cannot manage our relationships with people we lead until we are attuned to those people we are leading. If we are to skillfully manage our relationships, we will need to be able to manage the emotions of those we lead. When we empathize with people we begin to see things from their perspective. When we see things from their perspective we understand them and they feel cared for. When they feel cared for they will even do what they do not agree with. They will follow us because they want to. That, by the way, is the next to the highest level of leadership. The only level higher is when people follow you because they believe in your leadership.

It is important to say at this point, that simply doing emotionally intelligent things is not enough. We can use the tools and still fail. We can lean into people and be present, but we can do it with the motivation that they will think of us as a good leader, but they will not feel cared for or understood. We will need to see people differently. We will need to see them not as objects but as people with needs. I like how that was expressed by another writer. "One way, I experience myself as a person among people. The other way, I experience myself as the person among objects." The perfect example of this is when you have a heated argument with your spouse right before you leave home. You don't want to just leave, so you go and say, "I'm sorry," and lean over to give them a kiss. They know you don't mean it, and your kiss is nothing. Just as I mentioned earlier about the neurons, people know when what you are doing is using a new skill rather than seeking to do what is best for them. In "The Outward Mindset," by the Arbinger Institute, the writer says that we view people in one of three ways. "Those that can help me, I see as vehicles. Those that make things more difficult for me, I see as obstacles. Those whose help wouldn't matter become irrelevant to me." Eugene Peterson, in his book "The Unnecessary Pastor," says, "Martin Buber, in one of the most important books of the century for people like us, (meaning pastors) [entitled] 'I and Thou,' showed how easy and common it is to treat people as 'It' instead of as 'Thou.' He also showed how awful it is, turning what God created as a human community of men and women whose glory it is to love one another into a depersonalized wasteland of important roles and efficient function." If I am thinking about what I want, about my plans, my success, then people become objects. If I begin to see people with needs, wants, and dreams we begin to treat them differently. If we are making a presentation and thinking about how we will be received, what people will think about us or our presentation, we are thinking inwardly. The presentation is not about us. We are making a presentation to help people. Therefore, our focus should be on them. How can I help them? What do they need? I remember John Maxwell telling the story of a pastor who complained about "the ding-a-lings" in his church. That pastor left that church to find "ding-a-lings" in the next church. Here is a revolutionary thought: We are so convinced that the way we feel about certain people is because of the way they are. They have acted badly, treated us wrongly, or they have not done what they should do. But we see people the way we see them, not because that is the way they are, but because of the way we are. Stop seeing people as the problem and start seeing ourselves as the problem, and we will stop relating to them the way we have.

I made a startling discovery as I researched more and more about emotional intelligence and relating to others. In the church, we talk a great deal about holiness, and what it means to live a holy life. As I read about having a different mindset; not just learning skills, but seeing people with needs and desires just like myself, and not seeing them as objects, as instruments to accomplish my goals, a light came on. I realized, many of these things that I am finding in the business world are simply biblical principles of holiness. It is as Paul writes in Romans 12:2, "Don't copy the behavior and customs of this world, but let God transform you into a new person by changing the way you think." When I look at the life of Jesus I see how aware he was of himself. He knew when the woman with the issue of blood touched him. He said to his disciples in the Garden of Gethsemane how grieved he was. But he was always outward minded as well. He was always looking to meet the needs of others. He did not see people as objects to be used to attain his goals. He would see you, inspire you and make you want to do your best. I was always so consumed with trying to do whatever I could to get the church to grow, I did not see people and think about how could I help them. Without realizing it, I was seeing them as objects who would increase church numbers, help with ministry, and give tithes. Imagine what could happen if the Christian community began to see people, and began to ask, "What can I do to help?"

One conference, one book, or for that matter, several books, will not make us emotionally intelligent. There is not a 5 step plan that will immediately revolutionize your leadership. When I teach inductive Bible study and begin to tell students about making good observations, teaching them to identify structural relationships and ask interpretive questions; I tell them this takes practice. You will not get this right away. You will have to practice these things. But, the more you practice and keep it before you the better you will become. Your first sermon probably wasn't anything spectacular, but after years of writing sermons and preaching sermons your preaching is almost bearable. No matter how hard you study and work your IQ will not improve, but the more you practice and continue to learn, your EQ can improve and that will make a difference in you as a leader and in the people you lead.

You will want to especially look at the book "The Outward Minset" to learn more about being aware of others.

Arbinger Institute (2003). Outward Mindset. Oakland, CA. Berrett-Koehler Pub.

Dawn, M. & Peterson, E. (2000). The Unnecessary Pastor. Grand Rapids, Mich. Wm B. Eerdmans Pub.

Kubicek, J. (2015). 5 Gears: How to be present and productive when there is never enough time. Hoboken, NJ. Pub House.

SURVIVAL TIP #7

Be Aware of the Environment

During World War 2 the German army invaded Russia. They were eventually repulsed, in large part because they had not taken into consideration the climate of Russia. Their troops were not prepared for the harsh winter and many froze to death. It is important to take into consideration the environment of any destination. The same is true in other respects. We need to know the cultural climate of the church we are leading.

I am sure you are all to familiar with the ever present voices beating away at us, telling us as pastors that we need to go out and compete against the successful executives and entertainers who have made it to the top of their chosen professions, so that we can put our churches on the map and make it big in the religious world. This pressure also seems to come from within; from our congregations as well as from church leadership. Knowing who we are and realizing our success is not measured in size or quantity and knowing that we are supposed to be instilling and sustaining Christian character in the people we minister to can reduce some of that tension.

Our personal dysfunction contributes to make us the way we are. And while there is a part of that side of us that may be the thing that can help us succeed, it is also the less flattering side of us that can cause us the greatest problems when it comes to our relationships with others. Learning about some of that is not encouraging, but it makes us aware and can aid us in mitigating some of the fallout caused by our less savory aspects. It is not an excuse for our behavior, but it is a reason. We can do something about it.

Survival tips 5 & 6 were about looking at the need for knowing ourselves and leading ourselves because we cannot lead others if we cannot lead ourselves. And we need to be aware of others if we are to make them feel valued. John Maxwell says in James Kouzes and Barry Posner's book "Christian Reflections on the Leadership Challenge", "We need to work on ourselves before we work on others. We need to work more on ourselves than we work on others." Why is that? Because "people do what they see." So, using emotional intelligence and being outward minded we can effectively lead ourselves and then productively lead others. Having said that......

I read about a pastor who came to a church with fresh ideas and a clear vision of where the church could go. The church had not done much in many years, but he had not been there, and he was sure he could make a difference and things would be different since he was now the new sheriff in town. Does this sound vaguely familiar so far? After all, it was for those reasons the church called him. So he spent time and money taking the staff or church board members on a retreat to instill a new vision. He started new programs and changed the worship experience. They redecorated inside and out. They even created a great web page. But in 18 months the church was no better than they were when he came. What was wrong? He failed to understand the impact of the existing organizational culture. Samuel Chand, in "Cracking Your Church's Culture" says, "Culture—not vision or strategy—is the most powerful factor in any organization." He goes on to say that culture "determines the receptivity of staff and volunteers to new ideas, unleashes or dampens creativity, builds or erodes enthusiasm, and creates a sense of pride or deep discouragement about working or being involved there. Ultimately, the culture of an organization—particularly in churches and nonprofit organizations, but also in any organization—shapes individual morale, teamwork, effectiveness, and outcomes." Patrick Lencioni, in his book, "The Advantage," in the sub-title says, "organizational health trumps everything else...." Understanding church culture is critical to your survival as a pastor.

Another thing we probably were not taught in school is about our church culture. I had to chuckle as I read Gary McIntosh's book, "One Size Doesn't Fit All". After taking a church of 35 people he writes, "So there I sat, just six months into my first solo pastorate, struggling with the fact that I didn't know how to lead this small church into renewed growth and vitality. The things I learned in seminary—Christian education, biblical languages, homiletics, church history—while important foundations to my future ministry, had not provided me with the skills to lead this first small church."

What do I mean by culture? Ellen Wallach, a speaker, writer and filmmaker said, "Organizational culture is like pornography; it's hard to define, but you know it when you see it." When I hear that word the first thing that comes to my mind is Charles Emerson Winchester of Boston, Massachusetts, on the television program "M.A.S.H." He had culture in that he had refinement and social graces. He had a taste for what might be called the finer things in life. He preferred the opera to country music, filet mignon to fried chicken, and silk shirts to denim.

Culture can also mean people with different ethnicities; as well as from different times. I teach the book of Romans and the Synoptic Gospel's, and I tell my students that it is critical to understand the culture of first century Judaism and Christianity. They did not have a Western mindset and did not think and relate the same as we do in our Western culture.

Ferdinand Tonnies, in his book, "Community and Society," who lived from 1855 to 1936, came up with two basic types of organizations. He called them community, and society. The community organization is characterized by relationships, consensus, informality and kinship. Society, emphasizes relationships as being rational, formal, expedient and impersonal. Tonnies says, "All intimate, private, and exclusive living together, so we discover, is understood as life in community. Society is public life—it is the world itself. In community, with one's family, one lives from birth on, bound to it in health and prosperity, and in the times of hardship and sickness. One goes into society as one goes into a strange country. This is culture in its widest sense. This is the culture of where we live geographically and intimately. It is important to understand the culture of where you live. Then there is what is known as organizational culture. According to Max Weber in his book "The Theory of Social and Economic Organizations," there are three types of organizations: traditional, charismatic, and rational-legal. Already, you may be thinking how you did not realize there were these differences. Weber says that traditional organizations are formed on relationships and traditions and decisions are based on what has previously been done. We might characterize this as "This is the way we have always done it." You have probably heard that refrain where you serve. This is probably the organization culture of the majority of churches in America. Charismatic organizations are based on the "charisma" of the leader. Charisma simply means that the leader has a dynamic personality. In this type of organization decisions are made by the leader. There are some large churches that are what they are and do what they do based on the leader of that church. Therefore, since the leader is the center of the organization it does not continue without his leadership. The rational-legal organization makes decisions according to established procedures and policies, and responsibility is assigned by election. While Weber says there are just 3 basic organizational cultures, Dr. Charles Crow has done extensive study on church culture. He has discovered 4 church cultures and the behavior peculiarities within each culture. These different cultures are different in what they look like, what provides energy to the group, and who controls the decisions and resources. They plan differently and the kinds of programs in each culture will be different. Depending on the size of the organization, policies and procedures will be more or less extensive. There are many variables. I have included Dr. Crow's matrix at the back of this chapter. You will quickly be able to see your church and how it operates in the matrix.

So, let us look at what understanding culture can mean for you. I really liked Aubrey Malphurs definition of culture, in his book, "Look Before You Lead." He writes, "The church's congregational culture [is] the unique expression of the interaction of the church's shared beliefs and its values, which explains its behavior in general and displays its unique identity in particular." Edgar Schein, in "Organizational Psychology," defines it as: "A pattern of shared basic assumptions that the group learned as its problems of external adaptation and internal integration, that has worked well enough to be considered valid and, therefore, to be taught to new members as the correct way to perceive, think, and feel in relation to those problems."

Just as individuals are different, so are groups. We would never think of sending missionaries to a foreign country without first educating them concerning the culture of the people of that land. I grew up in South Florida and my parents were Yankees from New York, where I was born. My first church was in South Louisiana. That was nearly the same as moving to a foreign country. Even some of the language was different from what I was used to. You may recall the story of Boudreaux and Thibodeaux, and their peculiar way a talking, in a previous chapter. There were times I couldn't understand what people said. I later became good friends with Boudreaux and Thibodeaux and loved crawfish, red beans and rice, and jambalaya. The people were wonderful. However, I found that strangers were not quickly accepted and family units were very close. They did things differently than what I was accustomed to.

So why do we need to understand organizational church culture? We look at what churches do and those things are merely expressions. But why do they do those things? They do things based on their values, and their values come from their beliefs. There are several very compelling reasons to understand church culture. First, we need to understand the culture of the church because it exists within another culture in society. Just as you need to know yourself to lead yourself, you need to know your churches culture before you can impact the culture of the community outside the church. The American culture has greatly changed in the last fifty years. We have become pluralistic with many different views of spirituality. The Church is no longer the guiding influence that communities looked to for their moral direction. One writer says, America is "becoming an officially secular, pluralistic, and racially and ethnically heterogeneous society." The church often has not changed with the culture. I am not advocating we need to change our message and soften or dilute it in any way. I certainly would not advocate lowering the standard for holy living. The message of the church is needed more than ever; that is why we need to understand the culture of our church so we can proclaim the Gospel in a way that is in harmony with the culture of our community. I think back to when I came to my last church, which was located in a socio-economically poor community. The people were wonderful and hard working. They were not affluent or sophisticated by any means. I instructed the ushers to wear at least a tie on Sunday mornings. They were quite obliging and came the next Sunday morning in their finest attire. It only took the one Sunday for me to realize this was a bad idea and totally inappropriate for this culture. Other ministry ideas are not quite as obvious, but the results are the same.

Secondly, we need to understand church culture because we cannot minister in all cultures. We go to a church and think the people are nice and we look around and think about all we would like to do, but the culture of that church may be such that those things may be things that church will not implement. Too often, pastors go to lead an existing church, and they go not realizing that to do the things they want to do will mean changing the existing culture of that congregation. Church culture can be changed, and in many instances needs to be changed. However, it requires great patience and commitment. I think of a church that wanted to be a mission to the community by feeding the homeless and poor. They called a pastor and he came and wanted to stop one of the ministries they had been doing. Nobody said anything, but the attitude was, "That isn't going to happen." He was trying to create his culture rather than discovering the existing culture and working with that. He either was unaware or unwilling to invest the hard work and time to change the culture. Needless to say, he didn't last long at that church. If the pastor thought the church needed to change its culture perhaps he could have started by asking, "Why does the church have this ministry?" The answer may be that they value those people they are feeding. But why do they value them? Because they believe Jesus values them, and they believe that Jesus wants them to value them. Could there be another way to fulfill that belief? Could it be that the value could be changed? Yes, but that takes work and time. Changing culture is like Aesops Camel. "When man first saw the Camel, he was so frightened at his vast size that he ran away. After a time, perceiving the meekness and gentleness of the beast's temper, he summoned courage enough to approach him. Soon afterwards, observing that the animal altogether difficient (shy) in spirit, he assumed such boldness as to put a bridle in his mouth, and to let a child drive him." People are the same way about culture change. If a pastor can read the culture of a church, and his or her own culture, the better the chance that pastor will have of leading and ministering well in that culture. If we fail to read the culture, it will mean the culture of that church will lead and manage us. We need to understand that it is part of the job of the pastor to lead and manage congregational culture. But how can we do that if we don't understand our own culture as well as the church we are seeking to lead?

You do things that might be questioned as to the reason for doing them. You do them because you value something connected to that behavior. The reason you value that thing is because you believe something about it that is important. Why do you exercise? Because you value your health. You believe that exercising will improve your health. When people come to your church they are checking you out to see if this is a culture that they want to be a part. Does this church behave in a way that says they have the same values that we believe are important? Do they act in a way that that says the things we believe to be important are the same things the church sees as important? Behavior comes from values and values come from beliefs or "basic underlying assumptions." Edgar Schein says, "Basic assumptions are so taken for granted that for someone who does not hold them [that person] is viewed as crazy and automatically dismissed." Think about it like this: In Hebrew culture the group is more important than the individual. In Hebrew culture identity is found in the group and in relationship to others and not in themselves and their personal accomplishments. Therefore, the individual sacrifices for the good of the group. In Western culture the individual is honored over a group and the group is often asked to sacrifice for the good of the individual. The parents sacrifice their desires for the good of the child. Mark Strauss, concerning Hebrew culture, points out in his book "Four Portraits, One Jesus", "The goal for children in such a culture was not to make a better life than their parents', as often is the case in the West, but to guard the traditions, status, and honor of the family and to keep family bonds strong." The movie "Fiddler on the Roof" was about the father of five daughters, and his attempts to maintain his Jewish religious and cultural traditions as outside influences encroached upon the family's lives. These beliefs and values shape the behavior in a society just as they do in any culture. Churches have cultures where they have values they think are important. Not all of those values are appropriate or significant when it comes to the community.

Third, if we don't understand culture we will adopt the attitude, which is prevalent today of maintaining and surviving, and trying to keep the membership happy. As a leader, I found myself in a protection mode. For example, if there was a church down the road growing by leaps and bounds, I might point out how that church was seemingly selling a product rather than proclaiming the gospel. "Just look at their worship services. They are more entertainment than worship." Is that true, or did I just not understand my congregations culture? Aubrey Malphurs gives four other reasons for understanding culture. He says, "Culture shapes our lives and all our beliefs. Culture is vital to effective ministry. Our culture affects the way we conduct our ministries in the church, and culture lets us understand better the different people we seek to reach for Christ." That is why, while we need to know the culture of our community, for our purpose, we are referring to a different culture; organizational culture, and most particularly, church culture. Churches have a particular culture that needs to be understood. Every church has a unique culture. There are good cultures and bad cultures. I think back on the churches I served and all three were different from one another. The first was a mission church in what I would call a closed social environment. The second church was a church dominated by a single family. This is not a bad thing, but it is something that must be understood. My last church was in the heart of an economically challenged community. There was a history that went with the church. All of these churches had good things and all of them brought their own challenges. Had I known that I would have done things much differently.

I think, too often, the attitude has been that denominational leaders, educators and pastors see pastors as someone being sent by the denomination to particular churches, much as managers are sent by large corporations. Local churches see pastors as the person they have hired to help them accomplish their local goals and support their values, and because all local churches are different, it might be suggested that there could be a serious mismatch. In an article entitled "The Paradox of 'Corporate Culture': Reconciling Ourselves to Socialization," Richard Pascale said, "In fact, business schools find themselves in a particular dilemma since, in extolling management as a profession, they foster the view that a cadre of 'professional managers' can move from firm to firm with generic skills that enable them to be effective in each. This runs squarely against the requirements of a strong culture." You simply do not fit in every culture. Pascale defines socialization as "the process of being made a member of a group, learning the ropes, and being taught how one must communicate and interact to get things done." He goes on to quote Edgar Schein of MIT, who says, "I believe that management education, particularly graduate (business schools), are increasingly attempting to train professionals, and in the process are socializing the students to a set of professional values which are, in fact, in a severe and direct conflict with typical organizational values." I understand that the church is not a business and should not be run as such, but there are principles concerning the need for socialization. The best corporations thoroughly socialize new people while less successful companies do not. We too, need to learn the ropes on how things are done.

We move in and out of different cultures every day. There is a culture at home, where we work and at church. There may be an entirely different culture when we go play some sport. We act differently in each of those cultures. This is not being hypocritical, but understanding the acceptable ways of acting. I would submit that perhaps the same thing might be happening with clergy and their placement in churches. Pastors need socialization into the culture of the church when they come to lead it. We come to a church that already has an established culture and that culture is different from what we have come from or what we think it should be. It is the pastors job to lead the culture of their congregation, but if they do not understand that culture how can they lead it? I would also suggest that smaller churches tend to operate in Tonnie's "community" while larger churches operate in "society," which more closely matches what the denominations and the ministerial educational institutions value and teach. Pastors have been trained concerning the ideal way a church should operate and that is based on the corporate culture, as opposed to the family culture. The problem is that the greatest percentage of pastors will serve in a small church that operates completely different. This is a cause of conflict and frustration on the part of the pastor and the congregation.

Dr. Kenneth Crow, in a paper presented to the Association of Nazarene Sociologists and Researchers, entitled "Dynamics of the Placement Process," says, "Protestant clergy will mostly be pastors of small to mid-sized congregations—often in small town and rural areas where 52% of all congregations are located."

Researchers and theorists have compiled several lists of how churches compare. In other words, cultures display their unique identity in ways that include location, membership, program interests, relationship to the community, organizational characteristics, and size. I have included some of those descriptions in the Appendix 'D' on church culture.

When we look at organizational characteristics it is primarily the size of a congregation that determines its organizational characteristics. One chart I saw on church size categorized churches of 15-200 as small churches, 201-400 medium churches, and 401+ as large churches. Most of us would probably not consider 200 a small church, but that was divided into small, smaller and smallest. The smaller group was comprised of churches of 36-75. This group is also known as the "typical" church in size. Here is the interesting fact: 50% of all churches are smaller than the typical church. Small churches really operate more like a family while larger churches operate around a professional staff and organizational structure.

Dr. Charles Crow, several years ago, gave a perfect illustration of the differences in the culture of churches according to their size. He called it "The Zebedee Fishing Company." If you and a friend have a small boat and decide to go fishing, you really don't care if you catch any fish. What you want is the fellowship. Having a good time is the main objective. This would be characteristic of a small church. On the other hand, you may own a boat that is large enough to take groups out for a day of fishing. You want everyone to have a good time and to catch a few fish. The objective is to make a little money and to provide a service for others. This is characteristic of the medium size church. However, there are huge ships that troll the oceans hauling in tons of fish that must be cleaned packaged and kept in cold storage. The objective is to catch as much fish as possible in the shortest amount of time with the greatest efficiency. This is akin to the large church in structure and organization. While the objectives may not be the same when it comes to the various sized churches, the principle is the same. As you can see from all these different studies on church culture, it makes a huge difference on how things are done.

I conducted a survey of churches in my state and when questioned concerning Sunday worship attendance, this revealed that most of the pastor's served what would generally be classified as a small church. When I questioned those same pastors in regards to the organizational culture of their congregations, it showed that almost every pastor desired the church they were pastoring to operate like a medium to large size church. This demonstrates that many ministers do not understand the organizational culture of their congregations. Again, I have included the questions in the appendix 'E' from a paper by Dr. Charles Crow entitled "Operational Characteristics Evaluation: My Current Assignment" so you can evaluate your situation. There is also a helpful matrix in Appendix 'F' on church culture.

The point here is that church size has a great deal to do with its culture. However, let me reiterate that every church has a unique culture. Can we know the culture of a church? Can we understand the culture of the church we are serving? Yes, to all those questions. We also can change the culture of a church.

I think one question we have to ask is, "What kind of culture would I like in my church?" I recently read Robert Lewis and Wayne Cordeiro's book, Culture Shift". Wayne Cordeiro pastors a church in Hawaii. I guess someone has to serve there. He relates going to China to teach. In China Christianity is illegal. Eighteen people came to hear what he had to say. When asked how many people these 18 people in attendance oversaw, the answer came back about 22 million. When they were asked to read passages of Scripture many repeated them from memory because many of them had been imprisoned for their faith, and if they received some passage while in prison it would be confiscated. Therefore, they memorized any Scripture they came across. If these people were caught at this training they would be imprisoned and Wayne would be deported. 15 of these people had already gone to prison for their Christianity, and one had served 12 years for his beliefs. When the meeting was over, Wayne asked how he could pray for them. One man said, "Pray that we will become like you in America. You have many Bibles, freedom to worship openly, and even air conditioning to keep you from being distracted." Wayne said, "No. Instead, I will pray that we become like you." And everyone said, "Amen!" They have, in Wayne's words, "learned to incarnate a compelling, irresistible church culture." That is the desire of every pastor.

Earlier, I described what different church cultures look like and how they operate, but what makes church culture? It is not merely its size. Churches express their culture through their behaviors and outward appearances.

What we can observe is the expression of that culture. In teaching inductive Bible study, one of the steps in inductive work is observation. We can learn so much from the Bible by just making good observations. To be a good Bible student you need to be like a good crime scene detective. The more time spent in observation the less time is needed in interpretation, and the more likely your interpretation will be correct. By the same token, the less time spent in observation the more time will be needed in interpretation, and the less likely your interpretation will be correct. The same is true when it comes to understanding your church culture. I would say, make a minimum of 200 observations about your church. We can learn a great deal about a church by making thorough observations. Cordeiro calls those behaviors we can observe "totems". Native Americans created huge totems with animal designs. Each animal represented skills and values. These are visible things that tell of values. The behavior of a church reveals its values. Having said that, it is easier to observe the behavior than it is to understand why something is done, and why something isn't done. That involves values. It involves values in churches as well as in people. Churches and people act on their values. When we know what our values are, then, when behavior is contrary to those values we can redirect back to the values. When we do not live and act according to our values we create a culture that is dysfunctional. I think that much of what is done in the church is not value driven but performance and consumer driven. Why do we minister to people outside the church? Is it to get them to come to church? Or, is it because we value them and believe this is what Christ would have us to do? I heard about a pastor who had his church go to a large city function and hand out bottles of water with the church name on the bottles. When asked if the event was successful he replied, "Yes, but nobody came to church because of it." The question is: Did he do it to minister to people or to get them to come to church? But where do those values come from? As Malphurs says, "Churches are behavior-expressed, value-driven, and beliefs-based." I used to always say, "Show me your calendar and your checkbook and I will tell you what your priorities are." Find out what a church says about the past or the present and we know what it thinks about time. Discover how they see man as being good or bad and you will know what they believe about human nature. This is true about communication, power, tradition, finances, technology, and music. It is behavior, values and beliefs that make your church unique.

To discover those values will mean asking questions. In Bible study, we call these interpretive questions. They are the who, what, where, when, why and how in Bible study. In church culture study you need to ask questions about why people do what they do.

What really needs to be stressed is the need to understand your churches culture. There are great resources to help you uncover your churches culture. I would recommend "Look Before You Lead, by Aubrey Malphurs," first and the others in the bibliography afterwards. Once you have discovered your churches culture you can then begin to help it make the needed shifts to being a culture where both growth and birth spiritually and numerically can take place. I would say move slowly and bring people with you. I recently heard Jeremie Kubicek, the founder of Giant Worldwide, say that most successful people reach their peak performance between the ages of 55 and 70. If you aren't in that range you have however many years before you reach it. Don't try and rush the church through change. Pay the price of time.

Chand, S. (2011). *Cracking Your Church's Culture Code.* San Francisco, Ca. Jossey-Bass

Crow, C. (Nd.) *"Operational Characteristics Evaluation: My Current Assignment"* Matrix.

Crow, K. (2003). *Dynamics of the Placement Process.* Association of Nazarene Sociological Researchers.

Lewis, R. & Cordeiro, W. (2005). *Culture Shift.* San Francisco, Ca. Jossey-Bass

Malphurs, A. (2013). *Look Before You Lead.* Grand Rapids, Mich. Baker Books

Mcintosh, G. (1999). *One Size Doesn't Fit All.* Grand Rapids, Mich. Fleming H. Revell

Mcswain, L. (1980). "Community Forms and Urban Church Profiles. *Review And Expositor.* Ebscohost Accessed July 17, 2010

Pascale, R. (1995). *The Paradox of Corporate Culture: Reconciling Ourselves to Socialization, 6^Th Ed.* The Organizational Behavior Reader. Englewood Cliffs. Prentice Hall

Robinson, A. (2003). *Transforming Congregational Culture.* Grand Rapids, Mich. Wm. B. Eerdmans

Rothauge, A. (Nd.) *Sizing Up A Congregation for New Member Ministry.* Seabury

Schaller, L. (1975). *Hey, That's Our Church.* Nashville, Tenn. Abingdon

Schaller, L. (1985). *Middle-Sized Church: Problems And Prescriptions.* Nashville, Tenn. Abingdon Press.

Schein, E. (1974). *Organizational Pschology.* Englewood Cliffs. Prentice Hall.

Strauss, M. (2007). *Four Portraits, One Jesus.* Grand Rapids, Mich. Zondervan

Tonnies, F. (2002). Trans. Charles Loomis. *Community And Society.* Mineola. Dover

Weber, M. (1947). *The Theory of Social And Economic Organizations.* New York. Free Press

Some Final Thoughts

This book has been about many conversations I have had in regards to surviving as a pastor. But conversations are not deep studies. They are more like movie trailers to the movie itself. We catch a few scenes, but we do not see the whole movie. You have eavesdropped on these conversations, which is perfectly okay, and in fact it was what I hoped you would do. Hopefully, I have spoken loud enough so you did not have any trouble hearing. I hope that what you have read has piqued your curiosity and you will determine to learn more. I know you want to be the best pastor possible, and that is what I want for you too. It won't happen in one giant step or by reading a few books, but it could begin to make a difference as you integrate some of the material into your ministry.

Having been where you are I am all to painfully aware of your trials. I know you are not doing this for the money, power or prestige. If you thought that you would gain any of those things when you began you have long since come to the reality that those things are not going to come your way. You have spent hours alone weeping and wondering, that nobody ever will see or even know about. The real heroes in war are not those who come home, but those who die on the battlefield. You are spending your life on the hardest battlefield in the world. May God richly bless you.

I would like to hear from you and to learn if this book has been a catalyst to further study. Please email me at *michaelhurdman@yahoo.com*

Appendix A

Ihave borrowed heavily from Gary MacIntosh and
his assessments, but I created different questions to
help determine each dysfunctional behavior.

One of the things about being codependent is people
are drawn to you. You are a people pleaser. This is very common in ministry. You are so ready to do whatever people
want or need. Unfortunately, you may also resent people
for expecting so much out of you.

How do you know if you are a codependent leader?
To help you to understand if this is part of what shapes
your dark side I have included a short inventory. Read each
statement and circle the number that closest corresponds
to what describes you.

1 strongly disagree

2 disagree

3 uncertain

4 agree

5 strongly agree

1. I find it difficult to make decisions for fear that congregants will disapprove.

2. I find myself seeking the approval of superiors.

3. I find myself unwilling to confront bad behavior.

4. I get depressed if people do not want to follow leadership ideas.

5. I tend to allow others to make decisions rather than make them myself.

6. I find it difficult to express disagreement about things.

7. I find it difficult to initiate a project because of a lack of confidence.

8. I find it difficult to say 'No!' to people who want me to do things.

9. I fear appearing to be overconfident.

10. It bothers me if someone doesn't like me.

11. I need approval for my preaching.

12. I find that when I give in to other's requests of me I wish I had said, 'No!'

If you scored less than 20 you are probably not codependent. If you scored between 21 and 40 there is a good chance you have some codependent tendencies. If you scored more than 40 you are probably a codependent leader.

How do I know if I am an obsessive/compulsive leader. The great thing about compulsive leaders is they get things done. Once they get a hold of something they are like bulldogs. The reason bulldogs have their noses turned up is so they can bite something and hold on and it doesn't affect their breathing. Norman Shawchuck, in Leading the Congregation points out, "the compulsive leader desires to control everything and everyone in their lives. A fear of losing control drives them to desire a world in which everything is predictable and ordered." Obsessive, compulsive people are great at organizing, but they are terrible at allowing people to do projects without being controlled. Too often, the motto of the obsessive compulsive person is, "If you want it done right, you need to do it yourself." Compulsive leaders are generally over committed to work; they are workaholics. It shows itself in the pursuit of excellence as these leaders are often perfectionists. Gary MacIntosh points out Moses as a compulsive leader. If it had not been for his father-in-law, Moses would have worked himself to death. He was controlling every part of the life of an entire nation. He was spending all of his time "fixing" everyone's problems. Moses, when asked why he was doing this from morning to evening, says, "Because the people come to me to inquire of God; when they have a dispute, they come to me and I decide between one persona and another, and I make them know the statues of God and His laws."

The obsessive/compulsive leader is a controlling leader. Allender says, "The real goal of control is to eliminate chaos and uncertainty. But underneath all efforts to control is a reservoir of fear, and power is an antidote for fear. The controlling leader will appear far more confident and self-assured than what is actually the case. Underneath the façade the controlling leader is terrified." How do you know if you are an obsessive/compulsive leader? Read each statement and circle the number that closest corresponds to what describes you.

1 strongly disagree

2 disagree

3 uncertain

4 agree

5 strongly agree

---

1. I often worry that projects will go wrongly.

2. I have difficulty allowing people to do things the way they want.

3. There are times I cannot sleep because I can't stop thinking about something.

4. I need to have organized routine to life.

5. When things upset my routine it is frustrating.

6. I feel guilty if I take time off from work.

7. When things go wrong I get angry at little things.

8. I am angry if people don't do what I want them to do.

9. I am critical of work not done well.

10. I am aware of my status in relationships.

11. I find myself micromanaging projects and ministries.

12. I find myself thinking about work during leisure time.

If you scored less than 20 you are probably not obsessive/compulsive. If you scored between 21 and 40 there is a good chance you have some obsessive/compulsive tendencies. If you scored more than 40 you are probably an obsessive/compulsive leader.

David Goleman points out in "Social Intelligence," the narcissistic person has a "positive self-regard that gives...confidence appropriate to the ...level of talent—an essential ingredient for success. Lacking such self-confidence, people shrink from deploying whatever gifts or strengths they may have. Many narcissists are drawn to pressured, high-profile jobs where they can use their talents well and the potential laurels are great—despite any risks." He goes on to write, "The best creative strategists who can grasp the big picture and navigate risky challenges to leave a positive legacy."

One of the dysfunctions we think of being far from ministry is all too often very prevalent. The character MacIntosh describes is a real shock, when you think that he was also said to be the wisest man in the Bible. He writes, "Solomon reveals that he is obsessed with himself and with creating an image that would outshine the star of his revered father, David. Apparently, he succeeded, at least for a while. As a result of his massive, self-indulgent projects he began to feel temporarily satisfied with the image he had created for himself." How completely polar to this is what it means to be a godly leader? Allender writes, "But in God's economy, to be king means to be servant-shepherd. The terms king and shepherd were almost interchangeable in the ancient Near East. To be king meant to shepherd one's people from death to life." Many kings misunderstood or abused their calling and ended up devouring the flock—and then blamed the sheep for the dwindling numbers. Unfortunately, pastors treat churches and the people of the church as though they existed to make them successful. They would say they want the church to grow, but hidden beneath that, even unadmitted by the pastor, is the desire for a career to be promoted. Narcissism is marked by ambition and a zeal for bigger, better, and more, no matter what it costs the people. The narcissist craves admiration and they are driven to achieve.

This should be the opposite attitude of the pastor. As one writer says, "We should expect anyone who remains in a formal leadership context to experience repeated bouts of flight, doubt, surrender, and return. Why would this be God's plan? Why does God love the reluctant leader? Here is one reason: the reluctant leader is not easily seduced by power, pride, or ambition."

How do you know if you are a narcissistic leader? I have included a questionnaire to help you determine if you are. Read each statement and circle the number that closest corresponds to what describes you.

1   strongly disagree

2   disagree

3   uncertain

4   agree

5   strongly agree

---

1. Other leaders in the church often question my plans as being feasible.

2. When I hear about the successes of other pastors I get jealous.

3. I can envision myself as being a leader on a greater scale.

4. I like being recognized at meetings with my peers.

5. I often do not consider what something will cost to accomplish.

6. Even though I am doing better than many of my peers I still want more success.

7. I sometimes resent others and think I know what is best.

8. If a project fails it makes me feel like a failure.

9. I feel like I should have a larger congregation.

10. I am very conscious of how church leaders think about me.

11. I find it difficult to accept criticism.

12. I get angry when others question my decisions.

> *If you scored less than 20 you are probably not narcissistic. If you scored between 21 and 40 there is a good chance you have some narcissistic tendencies. If you scored more than 40 you are probably a narcissistic leader.*

The last of our dysfunctional leaders is the passive/ aggressive leader, or as the depressive leader. As I looked in the DSM5, I did not find this as an official psychological disorder, but came to find that it is a behavior that is more of a defense mechanism. I do think that Gary MacIntosh is right in assigning this dysfunction to Jonah. Norman Shawchuck describes the passive/aggressive leader as lacking initiative and confidence. This leader doesn't want to try anything too big for fear of failure. It also could mean that succeeding would carry with it the expectation to do even more, which they feel totally incapable of doing. The passive/aggressive leader uses procrastination as a norm. These leaders are prone to flying off the handle and losing their temper. They are also known for periods of sadness and repentance after such incidents. Depressive leaders are also complainers and are often impatient and irritable. They have a Dr. Jekyll/ Mr. Hyde way about them. People never know what they are going to be like. Consequently, being around this leader may make people feel uneasy. They never know when of why they may "go off." Finally, depressive leaders are pessimistic. They might say something like, "It won't do any good. These people are never going to change."

A passive-aggressive person is a nice person who intends to be good person but hurts others or himself without being aware of doing so and without being aware of the extent of repressed anger motivating his behaviors. Tardiness, pouting, procrastinating, being overly dependent, blaming others, and inefficiency are all passive-aggressive traits.(meierclinic.com) This may be a behavior many use unconsciously. Your spouse wants you to do something, but you don't do it. You have not done anything aggressively, but passively you have denied doing what you know is wanted.

How do you know if you are a passive/aggressive leader? I have included a questionnaire to help you determine if you are. Read each statement and circle the number that closest corresponds to what describes you.

1   strongly disagree
2   disagree
3   uncertain
4   agree
5   strongly agree

---

1. I find myself being late for meetings frequently.

2. When I am upset with someone I ignore their calls and messages.

3. I find myself procrastinating on things that need to be done.

4. I find myself complaining about my work.

5. When I want things done I don't ask directly.

6. I find myself not including certain people.

7. I find myself losing my temper.

8. When angry I give people the silent treatment.

9. I find myself to be generally pessimistic.

10. I try to get people to do things by making them feel guilty.

11. I sometimes don't attend functions where I am wanted.

12. I fear starting new project because they might fail.

If you scored less than 20 you are probably not passive/aggressive. If you scored between 21 and 40 there is a good chance you have some passive/aggressive tendencies. If you scored more than 40 you are probably a passive/aggressive leader.

Now that you are seeing your personality dysfunctions, perhaps it explains why you have had some of the problems you have experienced in ministry. However, none of this is an excuse for behavior that is detrimental to ministry. We may not be responsible for all the things that have gone into making us the people we are, but we are responsible for what we do with it. We are all dysfunctional to some degree, but we do not have to allow that dysfunction to sabotage our ministry and our relationships with others. We can be honest with ourselves and the people we are trying to lead and, as we realize dysfunctional behavior, take steps to correct that behavior.

In an article I read on emotional competency, the writer says, "Having responsibility is the duty or obligation to act. Taking responsibility is acknowledging and accepting the choices you have made, the actions you have taken, and the results they have led to. True autonomy leads to both having responsibility and taking responsibility. Taking responsibly is fulfilling your role in life. Responsibility is an essential element of integrity; it is the congruence of what you think, what you say, and what you do." As men and women of God, through the power of the Holy Spirit, we do not need to be controlled by our past. That certainly means in we do not need to be controlled by our past sins. It also means we do not need to be controlled by what has been done to us. We live in a victim dominated society. People want to blame someone or something for every bad thing in their life. There is a wonderful story told about a man who is out walking one night and comes upon another man down on his knees looking for something under a streetlamp. The passerby inquires as to what the other man is looking for. He answers that he is looking for his lost key. The passerby offers to help and gets down on his knees and helps him search for the key. After an hour of fruitless searching, he says, "We've looked everywhere for it and we haven't found it. Are you sure you lost it here?" The other man replies, "No, I lost it in my house, but there is more light out here under the streetlamp." We need to stop looking for other people and things to blame and take responsibility for ourselves. We need to stop making excuses for our failures. Excuses are, as someone said, just exits to success. I really like what Jack Canfield said in "The Success Principles." He writes, "Lots of people overcome these so-called limiting factors, so it can't be the limiting factors that limit you. It is not the external conditions and circumstances that stop you—it's you!" Perhaps, if we have seen some of these dysfunctional behaviors in our life we could confess them to the people we have been leading and take some specific remedial measures.

Appendix B

Below, is an emotional intelligence test. There are others that are available online, and if you purchase "Emotional Intelligence 2.0" a free test is provided. The test below was designed by Dr. Bob Kellerman, from rpmministries.org., in a March 7, 2011 article entitled, "Emotional Intelligence: The ABC's of Emotions, Part 6, How's Your Emotional Intelligence?"

1. I'm aware of my feelings and moods as they occur.

2. I'm able to recognize and name my feelings and moods.

3. I'm able to understand the causes of my feelings and moods.

4. I maintain a sense of ongoing attention to my internal mood states.

5. I'm aware both of my mood and my thoughts about my mood.

6. I actively monitor my moods as the first step in gaining control of them.

7. I soothe my soul in God—I candidly take my feelings and moods to Christ.

8. I have a sense of mastery—frustration, tolerance and anger management.

9. I self-regulate my emotions—self-control.

10. I can harness my emotions in the service of a godly goal.

11. I can stifle my impulses ("passions of the flesh") and delay gratification.

12. I'm a hopeful person.

13. I turn setbacks into comebacks.

14. I'm resilient and longsuffering. I demonstrate perseverance.

15. I practice Christ-centered hopefulness: "I can do all things through Christ who strengthens me." "I can meet the challenges as they arise." I'm competent in Christ."

16. I'm learning contentment in whatever state I'm in (external situation or internal mood).

17. I'm attuned to others, not emotionally tone-deaf. I have the ability to sense another's mood.

18. I have empathy built on self-awareness. I'm open to my own emotions and, therefore, skilled in reading the feelings of others.

19. I practice the creative ability of perceiving the subjective experiences of others.

20. I make another person's pain my own.

21. I can take on the perspective of another person.

22. I forgive.

23. I'm emotionally nourishing toward others.

24. I leave others in a good mood.

25. I'm effective in interpersonal relationships.

26. I help others to soothe their souls in their Savior.

27. I can initiate and coordinate the efforts of a group of people—helping them to move with synchrony and harmony.

28. I can negotiate solutions—mediation, preventing or resolving conflicts.

29. I can make personal connection—ease of entry into an encounter along with the ability to recognize and respond fittingly to people's feelings/concerns.

30. I'm skilled at social analysis—being able to detect and have insights into people's feelings, motives, and concerns. Ease of intimacy and rapport.

Appendix C

OPERATIONAL CHARACTERISTICS EVALUATION

MY CURRENT CHURCH ASSIGNMENT
*(Adapted from a paper by Dr. Charles Crow,
Dynamics of the Placement Process)*

The operation and management of churches can be described as including at least six functions: Planning, Organizing, Developing human resources, Budgeting, Supervising, Evaluating.

Not all churches carry out these functions in the same ways. The following scales are designed to describe operational characteristics of local churches. Using the one to ten scale provided, please indicate your observation of the particular church you are now serving. When completed, Appendix D is a Church behavior matrix to compare your answer and determine the culture characteristics of your church.

NOTE: *Describe what you observe in the church as it is, not as you think it should be. You will be asked to identify operational characteristics for your ideal church next.*

PLANNING

Planning involves determining needs, articulating goals, and making strategy or program decisions. Guiding the overall focus or purpose is included in the planning process.

Planning is used by organizations to think about or articulate desired results, and guide the activities and resource development necessary to achieve it. Churches range from informal work done by the group at every board meeting, to formal processes that are voted on by the board but remain easily changed, to highly structured processes with long range, mid range and immediate goals, objectives, and strategies.

Informal planning	1 2 3 4 5 6 7 8 9 10	Highly detailed planning

The process lacks a specified agenda	1 2 3 4 5 6 7 8 9 10	The process has a focused agenda

The process is open to with anybody able to participate	1 2 3 4 5 6 7 8 9 10	The process is assigned to particular persons who bring their recommendations to the board

The desired result is consensus	1 2 3 4 5 6 7 8 9 10	The desired result is a written document

Churches focus their planning on what seems to be most important to the ongoing life of the church. While there are many valid areas of focus, at one end of the scale would be building and maintaining relationships and at the other would be building and managing the church organization.

Building and maintaining relationships	1 2 3 4 5 6 7 8 9 10	Building and managing the church organization

Nurturing the persons already in the church	1 2 3 4 5 6 7 8 9 10	Evangelism and the growth of the church

Maintenance	1 2 3 4 5 6 7 8 9 10	Outreach

Spiritual Formation	1 2 3 4 5 6 7 8 9 10	Programs and events

Focused internally	1 2 3 4 5 6 7 8 9 10	Focused externally

ORGANIZING

Organizing involves setting up an organization and coordinating the activities to accomplish the goals and direction developed in the planning process.

Local churches organize their overall ministry in ways that give them an operational look and feel. At one end of the scale the church operates like a close knit family or club. At the other end the church operates more like a big university or business with well defined systems, a CEO and professionals making decisions. In the middle might be a family owned business set up to meet the needs of the family but also serving people outside of the family.

Close knit family/club	1 2 3 4 5 6 7 8 9 10	Big organizational enterprise

The organizational structure is simple like a family system with a patriarch or matriarch leader	1 2 3 4 5 6 7 8 9 10	The organization is complex with independent departments and directors who develop programs and activities which are brought to and authorized by the board

The way operational decisions are made in a particular church settles into a pretty predictable pattern. At one end of the scale, (major) decisions are made by a particular layperson who is the leader of the board and has the trust and support of the people. At the other end, the same decisions are made by the pastor or professional staff and enacted by the board with the trust and support of the people. In the middle there is a collaboration in which the board actually makes the decisions in the board meeting, usually after much discussion.

A particular layperson makes major decisions with trust and support	1 2 3 4 5 6 7 8 9 10	The pastor and/ or professional staff make decisions with board support and the people's trust

After discussion, the board looks to a board particular person for direction	1 2 3 4 5 6 7 8 9 10	After discussion, the looks to the pastor or a staff member for direction

The length of time particular persons have held power is another variable. In some churches the same persons/ families have held positions such as being board members for decades. The board positions may have been passed from one generation of a family to the next. At the other end of the scale the election process is designed to bring new persons and new thinking to these positions on a regular basis.

The same families Have run the board for decades	1 2 3 4 5 6 7 8 9 10	The board has been changing from year to year

The power structure is much the same as it was ten years ago	1 2 3 4 5 6 7 8 9 10	The power structure has changed significantly in the past ten years

DEVELOPING HUMAN RESOURCES

Developing human resources involves all of the processes of recruiting, training and empowering individuals to do the work that needs done. It includes paid staff and volunteers.

The role of the pastor at one end of the scale is to be a Chaplain, a friend to the patron, and to help maintain the church. In the middle, he/she is hired to be the manager of the church enterprise. Like the manager of a franchise, he/she is expected to run the enterprise for the leaders twenty four hours a day. Manager is the key word for understanding his/her role. At the other end, the pastor is hired to guide the expansive organization in much the same way as a corporate president. The pastor is no longer the manager of the day to day operation. Chief Executive Officer (CEO) is the key understanding of his/her role.

Pastor is Chaplain	1 2 3 4 5 6 7 8 9 10	Pastor is Chief Executive Officer

Churches with no permanent additional staff members are at one end of the scale. In the middle we find churches with staff. However, they tend treat the staff like assistants to the pastor rather than as independent professionals. At the other end staff members are hired as professionals in their field and given full responsibility to build their area of ministry.

No other paid staff	1 2 3 4 5 6 7 8 9 10	Full professional staff

Most of the work is done by volunteers however, at one end of the scale you have churches where everyone is expected to be involved in practically everything, and at the other end you have churches with highly specialized programs and activities with members being expected to be involved in at least one but not all of them.

Members are expected to volunteer to work in practically all areas of the life of the church	1 2 3 4 5 6 7 8 9 10	Members are expected to select areas of ministry for which they are particularly suited and olunteer to work in those programs or activities

It is assumed that the same people will volunteer for the same programs year after year   1 2 3 4 5 6 7 8 9 10   Volunteers are specifically recruited for each cycle of a program or activity, providing an opportunity for new workers

ob descriptions and performance expectations are not provided in written form   1 2 3 4 5 6 7 8 9 10   Detailed job descriptions with performance expectations are provided to each worker prior to accepting the assignment

Training for volunteers is informal and often done "on the job"   1 2 3 4 5 6 7 8 9 10   Training for volunteers is formal and done prior to the program or activity

BUDGETING

Budgeting involves the development of resources (funding) as well as the allocation and management (spending) of those resources. This would include facilities, equipment and money.

A budget is a tool by which persons, groups, and organizations plan their expenditures for the coming year. At one end of the scale a budget would be very informal with expenditures being tied to what was available, or sometimes the amount of money raised would be tied to necessary expenditures. The leading layperson ultimately makes decisions about what will be spent. In the middle of the scale we find churches that set up a budget at the beginning of the year and then go ahead and spend money as it is available and necessary rather than follow the budget closely. At the other end of the scale we find a very formal budget prepared by the pastor and/or professional staff and based on specified program needs as well as carefully analyzed income projections.

| No formal budget | 1 2 3 4 5 6 7 8 9 10 | Very formal budget |

| In the absence of a formal budget process, the leading layperson determines spending | 1 2 3 4 5 6 7 8 9 10 | The pastor or administrator guides the professional staff in the development of a detailed budget which is adopted by the board |

Sources of funding for the budget may influence the allocation of budget spending items. That is to say, the relationship between the amount of money a person or family gives and the power that they have in the church is not the same in all churches.

| The power structure reflects how much money is being or haas been given | 1 2 3 4 5 6 7 8 9 10 | The power structure doesn't reflect the giving patterns of the various families in the church |

A high percentage of the total raised each year is given by members of the board	1 2 3 4 5 6 7 8 9 10	A low percentage of the total raised each year is given by members of the board

The role of the treasurer varies from church to church. At one end of the scale, the treasurer protects the leading layperson by exercising strong control over what is spent and what it is spent on. In the middle he/she has about the same voice as anyone else on the board, and at the other end, he/she functions as a bookkeeper or accountant providing very detailed reports to the board/staff with actual spending compared to budgeted spending.

The treasurer functions as a controller	1 2 3 4 5 6 7 8 9 10	The treasurer functions as an accountant

The treasurer does the accounting personally and prepares his/her own reports for the board meeting	1 2 3 4 5 6 7 8 9 10	A paid secretary or bookkeeper does the accounting at the church and prepares reports for the treasurer to take to the board meeting.

The sense of ownership of church property extends along a continuum also. At one end the congregation is experienced as an extension of the family and all church property, including the church building, is more or less an extension of family property. Every adult has a key to the building and equipment is frequently taken home for personal use. At the other end church property belongs to the church. Only officers and staff are to have keys.

Church property is an extension of personal or family property	1 2 3 4 5 6 7 8 9 10	Church property is corporate property and not to be taken for personal use

SUPERVISING

Supervising involves the managerial role of overseeing the work of others as well as ongoing support, encouragement, and skill development.

The supervision process is informal with most members feeling freeto encourage and/or criticize others	1 2 3 4 5 6 7 8 9 10	Supervision is very structured with program directors responsible for overseeing the activities of the workers in their departments

Performance evaluation is informal	1 2 3 4 5 6 7 8 9 10	Performance evaluation is formal

Performance evaluation is not based on the job description	1 2 3 4 5 6 7 8 9 10	Performance evaluation is based on the job description

Information about performance is communicated throughout the group without fear of "going over someone's head"	1 2 3 4 5 6 7 8 9 10	Information about performance is communicated confidentially through proper channels to the proper persons for appropriate action

Everyone has easy access to the pastor and all of the church leaders	1 2 3 4 5 6 7 8 9 10	A limited number of people have easy access to the pastor and all of the church leaders

Conflicts are resolved by the group	1 2 3 4 5 6 7 8 9 10	Conflicts are resolved by supervisor or program director

At one end of the scale, there are churches who regard continuing education for the pastor to be unnecessary. If he/she wants to take a week long class at the regional college or university it is viewed as a waste of time. If he/she actually takes the class it is done at the pastor's own expense. At the other end, continuing education is encouraged and both time and money are provided.

Continuing education is at the pastors' time off & expense	1 2 3 4 5 6 7 8 9 10	Continuing education is encouraged with time and money provided

A similar range of attitudes exists related to continuing training for volunteers in the programs and activities of the church.

| Continuing train-ing pretty much left up to the individual | 1 2 3 4 5 6 7 8 9 10 | Training events and volunteer staff meetings are held on a regular schedule |

Policies are used in organizations to supervise or control the way things are done. Churches range from no written policies, to informal, to formal but not enforced, to highly structured and carefully followed.

| No written policies | 1 2 3 4 5 6 7 8 9 10 | Policies structured and followed |

EVALUATING

Evaluation is used to determine if the desired results are being achieved, and to determine what plans need to be changed.

Evaluation is used by organizations to determine whether the activities and programs are achieving the results they articulated in the planning stage. Churches range from informal work done by the group at every board meeting, to formal processes that are voted on by the board but remain easily changed, to highly structured processes with a written document articulating how the actual results compare with the long range, mid range and immediate goals, objectives, and strategies.

Evaluation is informal and ongoing	1 2 3 4 5 6 7 8 9 10	Formal evaluations are conducted at preset times

Evaluation does not product a formal report with recommendations for approval	1 2 3 4 5 6 7 8 9 10	Evaluation produces a detailed written report with specific recommendations for board approval

Anyone can evaluate any part of the program at any time	1 2 3 4 5 6 7 8 9 10	The board appoints selected persons to evaluate particular programs at specified times

Program evaluation is based on how the leaders "feel"	1 2 3 4 5 6 7 8 9 10	Program evaluation is carefully based on pre-determined outcome criteria
Program evaluation is based "feelings" about the results	1 2 3 4 5 6 7 8 9 10	Program evaluation is carefully based on pre-determined outcome criteria
Statistical information is kept more for reporting to the denomination than for internal evaluation	1 2 3 4 5 6 7 8 9 10	Statistical information is kept more for internal evaluation than for reporting to the denomination
Program evaluation is based on how the leaders "feel" about the results	1 2 3 4 5 6 7 8 9 10	Program evaluation is carefully based on pre-determined outcome criteria

Ongoing informal evaluation without formal recommendations or approval	1 2 3 4 5 6 7 8 9 10	Regular evaluations at preset times with recommended changes to plans being formally approved and program changes being made

What is the approximate seating capacity of your sanctuary? _____

_____

_____

What did you report as your average morning worship attendance last year? _____

_____

_____

_____

MY IDEAL CHURCH

Directions: You have just completed a set of scales about the church you are serving. Would you please use the same scales to describe the ideal church you would like to pastor someday.

| Close knit family/club | 1 2 3 4 5 6 7 8 9 10 | Big organizational enterprise |

| Communication is informal and facepublic to face | 1 2 3 4 5 6 7 8 9 10 | Communication is formal, an- nouncements, memos, bul- letins, and news letters |

| Building and maintaining relationships | 1 2 3 4 5 6 7 8 9 10 | Building and managing the church organization |

| People want to know each other in almost every area of their areas of life or by the lives | 1 2 3 4 5 6 7 8 9 10 | People have close friends but are content to know most other mem- bers in limited church lives posi- tions they have in the church |

| Decisions are made for the good of the church "family" | 1 2 3 4 5 6 7 8 9 10 | Decisions are made for the good of the church organization |

| Nurturing the persons already in the church | 1 2 3 4 5 6 7 8 9 10 | Evangelism and the growth of the church |

| Maintenance | 1 2 3 4 5 6 7 8 9 10 | Outreach |

| Spiritual Formation | 1 2 3 4 5 6 7 8 9 10 | Programs and events |

| Focused internally | 1 2 3 4 5 6 7 8 9 10 | Focused externally |

Most church events can be altered to accommodate (e.g. worship) the wedding of church events members' children

1 2 3 4 5 6 7 8 9 10

Even member weddings are scheduled around the public (e.g. worship) (e.g. Saturday night weddings are not allowed)

A particular layperson makes major decisions with trust and support

1 2 3 4 5 6 7 8 9 10

The pastor and/or professional staff make decisions with board support and the people's trust

After discussion, the board looks to a particular person for direction

1 2 3 4 5 6 7 8 9 10

After discussion, the board looks to the pastor or a staff member for direction

The same families have run the board for decades	1 2 3 4 5 6 7 8 9 10	The basic make up of the board has been changing from year to year

The power structure is much the same as it was ten years ago	1 2 3 4 5 6 7 8 9 10	The power structure has changed significantly in the past ten years

The power structure reflects how much money is being or has been given	1 2 3 4 5 6 7 8 9 10	The power structure doesn't reflect the giving patterns of the various families in the church

No formal budget	1 2 3 4 5 6 7 8 9 10	Very formal budget

The treasurer functions as a controller	1 2 3 4 5 6 7 8 9 10	The treasurer functions as an accountant
Church board operates as a unit	1 2 3 4 5 6 7 8 9 10	Church board accepts or rejects the recommendations of committees
The organizational structure is simple & like a family it doesn't change much from year to year	1 2 3 4 5 6 7 8 9 10	The organization is structured into committees that work independently and guide the changes brought to and authorized by the board
Everyone has easy access to the pastor and all of the church leaders	1 2 3 4 5 6 7 8 9 10	A limited number of people have easy access to the pastor and all of the church leaders

No written policies	1 2 3 4 5 6 7 8 9 10	Policies structured and followed

Informal planning	1 2 3 4 5 6 7 8 9 10	Highly detailed planning process

Ongoing informal evaluation without formal recommendations or approval	1 2 3 4 5 6 7 8 9 10	Regular evaluations at preset times with recommended changes to plans being formally approved and program changes being made

Church property is an extension of personal property or family property	1 2 3 4 5 6 7 8 9 10	Church property is corporate and not to be taken for personal use

_____

| Pastor is Chaplin | 1 2 3 4 5 6 7 8 9 10 | Pastor is Chief Executive Officer |

_____

| No other paid staff | 1 2 3 4 5 6 7 8 9 10 | Full professional staff |

_____

| Continuing education is at the pastors' time off & expense | 1 2 3 4 5 6 7 8 9 10 | Continuing education is encouraged with time and money provided |

_____

In your ideal church, how many would the sanctuary seat? _____

_____

_____

What would be the average morning worship attendance? _____

_____

_____

Appendix D

Lyle Schaller in his book, "Hey, That's Our Church," describes six models of churches and two of the models are based on location. The "Ex-neighborhood Church," is the church that was started to serve a neighborhood made up primarily of the same kind of people. However, as time passed and the original members died or moved, it left the church with a large percentage of people who did not live in the neighborhood, but were loyal because it was their home church. This church may still be alive, but it is no longer made up of the same kind of people and that is what had given it its identity.

Then there is the "Ex-rural Church," which was started in a rural area where it reflected the values and lifestyles of rural or small town people. But the city grew and engulfed the church, surrounding it with families with different values. This church will either change or become defensive and not grow.

Again, Schaller describes what he calls "Saturday Evening Post Churches." These churches are based on the magazine by the same name in that they offer "something for everyone." This type of church could be described as nostalgic for it keeps the same programs that have been popular with its members in the past. Its membership is largely over the age of forty and usually has little appeal to younger people.

Churches often start out reflecting the values and characteristic of the community they are in. However, as the community changes the amount of involvement by the church in the community may also change.

Larry McSwain developed a set of descriptive profiles involving three broad categories of churches.

There is the "Communal Group" which, is made up of all kinds of people who are like minded in their faith. These groups have close friendships and common interests that make them strong, but because of their inward focus they tend to have limited interaction with the community. He says there are four types of churches in this group. They are: the house church, the storefront church, the ethnic church and the special purpose church.

Then, there is the "Neighborhood Church." The people in these churches either live within a two mile radius of the church, or they lived within that geographical area when they joined the church. McSwain says there are seven types of neighborhood churches. They are: the midtown congregation, the inner-city congregation, the inner-urban neighborhood, the outer-urban neighborhood, the city suburb church, the metropolitan suburb church and the rapidly growing suburban church.

It is the Neighborhood Church that is most involved in the community, and because of that, if they do not keep up with what is going on in the community it will greatly affect the church.

Finally, there is the "Multi-Neighborhood Church." This is a large church with a membership in the thousands and is able to support a large staff and has a wide variety of programs. These churches are highly consumer-oriented in their approach is using television, radio and other media to reach out. He lists two such churches and one of them is the Old First Church, which may be a large cathedral and the metropolitan regional church, which is like old first church except it is located on a major thoroughfare and is a newer congregation.

McSwain describes the "Multi-Neighborhood Church" as having a large staff with a variety of programs. Because of this it needs a staff that can be responsible for individual areas.

Arlin Rothauge shows how the operational characteristics change as the size of the congregation changes. He says, "The size of a congregation acts as a key variable in those factors that determine the structure, functions, and style of relationships in its group life." He uses the average attendance at worship over a one year period to determine the size of a church. A church of up to fifty people is called a "Family Church." It has the characteristics of a family with strong parental figures who are in control of family life. When there is harmony in the church, this size congregation offers a family type support and there is a great sense of belonging.

The medium size church consists of between 50 and 150 in attendance and is called a "Pastoral Church." Because it is larger than the family church it requires more professional type leadership. This type of leadership replaces the patriarchal and matriarchal leadership of the family church.

The large church has 150 to 350 people in attendance and it is called the "Program Church." This size church requires a more democratic style of organization because it is not possible for a single leader to stay in contact with the entire congregation. The major decisions are made by some sort of a representative governing body. The clergy serves more in administrative activities such as coordinating the different ministries.

The church with more than 350 members is the extra large church and is called the Corporation Church. This size church is an even more complex organization. Rothauge says, "The head pastor becomes a symbol of unity and stability in a very complicated congregation life. The leadership of the laity now takes a multi-level form in which there is opportunity for working up the ladder of influence in the large community. We see the outline of the program church, but with more divisions of activity and more layers of leadership ranks."

Appendix E
CHARLES CROW MATRIX

CHARLES CROW MATRIX

	BASIC FAMILY (1-50)	EXTENDED FAMILY (51-150)	FAMILY ENTERPRISE (151-350)	CORPORATE ENTERPRISE (350+)
FOCUS[1]	Looks like a family. Limited number of participants allows each to know every other participant very well. (¶ 44)	Looks more like a family reunion. Three or four family leaders have emerged to run things for the family. (¶ 89)	Looks like a business owned and operated by a family to meet the needs of the family by reaching outside the family. The focus has shifted from internal to external. This church wants to accomplish more than just meeting the needs of the family of participants. (¶ 131) Still under the control of a family coalition. Specific families have controlled the leadership positions for a long time. (¶ 131)	Hierarchical in structure with specified levels of authority in a series of levels that resemble a pyramid with the senior pastor at the top. (¶ 174) Written rules and policies guide nearly every aspect of the management of the organization. (¶175) Management is a full time vs. secondary activity. (¶ 177)
	Relationships provide the driving energy for the organization; i.e., the church is successful when the relationships are good. (¶ 49)	Driving energy is the responsibilities within the relationships. Apt to divide up the work load and relate to each other in overlapping roles. (¶ 94)	Focuses on building and managing the organization, perhaps establishing status denominationally. Long term staff, in addition to the pastor. (¶ 136)	Driving energy is worship. (¶ 181) Supports the denomination rather than drawing from the denomination; has a life of its own that seems to exist beyond the denomination. (¶ 180)
	Theme song: "You may notice we say brother and sister 'round here. It's because we're a family and these folks are so dear." (¶ 48)	Theme song: "I'm so glad I'm a part of the family of God." (¶ 92)	Not knowing everybody in the church is an ongoing source of frustration. (¶ 137)	Not knowing everybody is an accepted reality. From the intentional changing of the makeup of the board to the freedom to participate in programs without joining any membership list, this church is a very open system. (¶ 190)

1) The entire source file for this matrix can be found as http://nazarene.org/files/docs/Enduring%20Cultures%20of%20Laity.pdf
Dr. Charles Crow - charlescrow@outlook.com

	BASIC FAMILY (1-50)	EXTENDED FAMILY (51-150)	FAMILY ENTERPRISE (151-350)	CORPORATE ENTERPRISE (350+)
PLANNING	Patron/matron provides and controls most operational resources; provides stability; is the primary stakeholder. (¶ 53-54) Patron/matron can override official church board decisions. (¶ 50)	Dominant coalition is made up of the husband/wife teams of a small group of families, usually three or four. Planning looks like planning done by families. Plans have emerged over many years, and the church has reflected the stability of those plans. (¶ 99)	Guiding coalition is made up of four or more families that have served the church for multiple generations. The church is perceived by the guiding coalition as existing to serve the spiritual needs of the families of the church and the community about equally. (¶ 139)	Guiding coalition is a somewhat fluid group with the pastor as the CEO type of leader. Persons in guiding coali-tion will be influential in decision making but may not have held their position for any great length of time. (¶ 183) Most leadership and day to day management comes from the pastor and staff. Board is elected every year. Many of these churches impose a limit on years of continuous service. (¶ 184)
	Informal planning. (¶ 50)	Informal planning. (¶ 96)	Formal planning that remains flexible. (¶ 138)	Formal planning, with some flexibility, designed to carry plans and processes from one leadership group to the next. (¶ 182)
	Informal goals are meaningful to the patron/matron (¶ 52).	Needs are assumed rather than being formally assessed by the leaders. (¶ 97)	Needs assessed each year as a specific action of the board, but without broadly spread participation in the collection of information. Part of the reevaluation of the long-range plan; forms the basis of how to act when particular needs become urgent but does not initiate action. (¶ 141)	
	Patron/matron is able to respond to changing needs and opportunities. However, basic plan to care for, and protect the family will not change much from year to year. (¶ 53)	While planning is not formal or long range, the guiding coalition is very quick to respond to changes or sudden needs. When faced with a task or problem to be solved, these leaders are capable planners and problem solvers. (¶ 98)	Guiding coalition is quick to respond to the needs of the families and the church family as a whole.	

	BASIC FAMILY (1-50)	EXTENDED FAMILY (51-150)	FAMILY ENTERPRISE (151-350)	CORPORATE ENTERPRISE (350+)
ORGANIZING	Organized informally to accomplish informal goals. (¶ 55)	Organized informally to accomplish informal goals. (¶ 100)	Departmental structure. (¶ 142)	Departments officially outlined and governed by the rules and policies established by the board. (¶ 173) Professionals, hired in each area, are charged with the development of programs and processes to accomplish the objectives of the master plan. (¶ 187)
			Everyone has direct access to the leadership of the church. (¶ 143)	Most participants relate to the structure through program directors and group leaders. (¶ 188)
	Limited resources focused on general activities. (¶ 57)	Programs designed to be general in nature, requiring little training for the participants. (¶ 101)	New programs initiated nearly every year, but core activities remain relatively unchanged for many years. (¶ 143)	
	Programs center around fellowship and worship. (¶ 58)	Programs, based on the way things have been done in the past, center around fellowship and worship. (¶ 101)	Programs center around fellowship and worship; however, worship is probably the more important of the two. (¶ 145)	Events provide the driving energy. (¶ 181) Worship is the one activity considered common to all participants. (¶ 190)
	Activities designed so that everyone will participate in everything; spiritual commitment and growth evaluated on the basis of complete participation. (¶ 58)	Most people are expected to participate in most programs and activities. (¶ 101)	Attempt to structure activities in general ways so that nearly everyone can be involved in nearly everything. (¶ 143)	Events and activities are for specialized groups of people; not designed to involve every one. Participants select the groups and activities that fit their personal growth needs; not expected to participate in all activities. (¶ 189)

	BASIC FAMILY (1-50)	EXTENDED FAMILY (51-150)	FAMILY ENTERPRISE (151-350)	CORPORATE ENTERPRISE (350+)
ORGANIZING *(cont.)*	No written polices or procedures; not regarded as necessary. Everyone in the family understands the way things are done. (¶ 59)	Procedures and policies exist in the collective memory of the group; not written or formal. Disputes about procedures and policies are settled by the guiding coalition, based on their personal memory of how things are done here. (¶ 102)	Procedures and policies are written but not followed by the leaders. Policies may be in place to control persons who are not on the board or part of the leadership coalition. (¶ 146)	Well-developed operations manual. Policies and procedures are the basis for how things happen; not in place to control certain individuals. Policies reviewed on an ongoing basis. Great care taken to insure that the manual remains consumer oriented rather than control oriented. (¶ 191)
	Power vested in the patron/matron; the pastor does not possess power. (¶ 60)	Church is large enough that one person cannot control everything. (¶ 95) Power vested the dominant coalition—a small group of patrons or matrons. Key leadership positions have been in the hands of the same families for two and even three generations. (¶ 103) Intergroup conflict (politics) about the operation of the church is often a source of family dysfunction. (¶ 95)	Power vested in an expanded group of patrons or matrons. Key leadership positions have been in the hands of the same families for two and even three generations. A key source of stability; often becomes a source of conflict. (¶ 147)	Power vested in the pastor with the specific backing of those who would have the power if there were no pastor. (¶ 192)
	Authority located in the family. Family gives the patron/matron the power based on a long history of being able to provide workable solutions to the problems facing the group. (¶ 61)	Authority located in the family, but delegated to the church board. With a long history of providing workable solutions to the problems facing the group, church board is generally trusted to make sure that the decision the family has made outside of the board meeting will be carried out by the pastor and church leaders. (¶ 104)	Authority located in the board and shared to some extent with the pastor. In most cases the group has some history of looking to the pastor for providing workable solutions to the problems facing the group. (¶ 148)	Authority located in the pastor and professional staff. (¶ 193) Authority within the structure is clearly spelled out in job descriptions. (¶ 173)

	BASIC FAMILY (1-50)	EXTENDED FAMILY (51-150)	FAMILY ENTERPRISE (151-350)	CORPORATE ENTERPRISE (350+)
ORGANIZING (Cont.)	Decisions made by consensus with leadership from or direction by the patron/matron. (¶ 62)	Decisions made like the basic family church but with an added step: Patron group reaches consensus before giving direction to the larger group (¶ 105)	Decisions made by the board with input from the pastor. (¶ 149)	Decisions made by the board with input from the pastor. (¶ 194) The function of the board is to set policy and provide support and oversight. (¶ 184)
	No committees, though the congregation may function as committee of the whole. (¶ 63)	Few committees since most of the involved people would be on most committees anyway. However, some people are primarily concerned with only one area or another. (¶ 107)	Church board typically organized into committees. Committees end up functioning like fact-finding task forces. Board rediscusses the entire problem rather than voting to accept or reject the committee recommendation. (¶ 150)	Church board typically organized into committees. Board receives committee report and, with opportunity for discussion, votes to accept or reject the recommendation, or to refer an item back to the committee for more work. (¶ 195)
	Basis of decision: "What is best for the family." (¶ 62)	Basis of decision: "What is best for this church family [clan]." (¶ 105)	Basis of decision: "What is best for the church." Success of the church is regarded as more important than individual desires. (¶ 149)	Basis of decision: "What is best for the church." Success of the church is regarded as more important than individual desires. (¶ 194)
	Enacting change requires group consensus and ultimately the patron/matron's permission. (¶ 64)	Enacting change requires the permission of the dominant coalition. (¶ 108)	Enacting change requires a decision of the board, which may have a tendency to micro manage the operation. (¶ 151)	Enacting change requires permission of the pastor. The role of the board is to see that the decision the pastor has made gets carried out. (¶ 197)
	Church property/building seen as extension of personal/family property. Every adult has a key to the building. (¶ 65)	Church property/building seen as extension of personal/family property. Not everyone has a key but for those who have been there long enough, the church property is their property to use. (¶ 109)	Church property/building viewed as a resource for building the enterprise. Most persons do not have keys and equipment is reserved for church use. (¶ 152)	Equipment is purchased and maintained by individual departments. Use arrangements must be made in advance. (¶ 198) Only officers and staff have keys. Staff members may not have keys to each other's areas. Few master keys are in existence. (¶ 199)

	BASIC FAMILY (1-50)	EXTENDED FAMILY (51-150)	FAMILY ENTERPRISE (151-350)	CORPORATE ENTERPRISE (350+)
DEVELOPING HUMAN RESOURCES	Volunteers are the human resource. Even the pastor may be bivocational. (¶66)	With the exception of the pastor, all human resources are volunteers. (¶110)	Most of the human resources are volunteers, but some paid staff (e.g., secretary, youth pastor, part time music minister). (¶153)	Most of human resources are volunteers; all programs and activities come under the oversight of a paid staff person. (¶200)
	Program is based on necessity, not design; is simple; the same people have been doing the same jobs for quite some time. (¶67)	Volunteer-run programs are general in nature; require little training. Skills learned through years of participating in the same activities. Some eventually become leader of some activities. (¶111)	Intention to keep programs general so that most people can be involved without the necessity of special training. (¶154)	Individuals holding positions have special training for their jobs. (¶176)
	Pastor recruits, but motivation for volunteering comes from the group rather than the pastor. (¶68)	Volunteering is an assumed role of church participants; recruiting is informal (e.g., an announcement about what needs to be done). (¶110) The pastor is responsible to assure an adequate number of volunteers, but motivation for volunteering comes from the group rather than the pastor. (¶112)	Workers recruited by announcing the need, and asking for volunteers. (¶154) Few jobs are regarded as one-time assignments. Workers are reasonably aware that they will informally be expected to volunteer for their assignment again and again. (¶156)	Volunteers recruited for specific positions and provided with a written job description for that position. Agree to certain lengths of service with the ability to drop out if necessary. Revolunteering is encouraged, but not definitely expected. Sabbaticals common and encouraged. (¶203)
	Family social networks form the basis of how work teams (e.g., funeral meals) develop. (¶69)	Work teams are based on the informal social networks rather than skills and abilities. (¶113)		Many volunteers find their fellowship needs met within the group of persons involved in their same program area so they tend to remain active until other responsibilities draw them away. (¶203)

	BASIC FAMILY (1-50)	EXTENDED FAMILY (51-150)	FAMILY ENTERPRISE (151-350)	CORPORATE ENTERPRISE (350+)
DEVELOPING HUMAN RESOURCES *(cont.)*	No formal personnel policies. No written job descriptions. (¶70)	No formal personnel policies. No written job descriptions. (¶114)	Development of human resources is formal; i.e., when people volunteer for most activities, they are given a written job description. (¶154)	All staff, paid and volunteer, have job descriptions. (¶201) Authority within the structure is clearly spelled out in job descriptions. (¶173)
	Everyone is informally accountable to everyone else; like a family, they guide and motivate each other to at least adequate performance and compliance with assumed responsibilities. (¶70)	Everyone is informally accountable to everyone else; like a family, they guide and motivate each other to at least adequate performance and compliance with assumed responsibilities. (¶114)	Recognition of workers is formally done in some of the programs with presentation of certificates, plaques, and awards often at a banquet. (¶155)	Recognition of workers is formally done in some of the program areas and informally done in others. (¶202)
	Pastor is hired to maintain the family property (church), service the family [chaplain], and be a friend to the patron/matron. (¶72)	Pastor is hired to help the guiding coalition in its tasks of maintaining the family property (church), servicing the family [chaplain], keeping within the budget, and being a friend to the leaders. (¶116)	Pastor is responsible for the operation of the church on a twenty-four-hour basis. Manager is the key descriptive word. More like the acting director of an agency or a franchise manager than a chief executive officer of a corporation. Responsibilities include making sure the doors are unlocked and locked at the appropriate times as well as supervising every committee and department. Staff members are viewed as his assistants, and he is responsible to supervise their work and behavior. In addition, s/he must see to the spiritual welfare of the members [chaplain]. (¶157)	The role of the pastor is like the chief executive officer of a corporation. Active in the day to day operation, but most specifically charged with providing vision and direction to the organization. (¶204) To be successful the pastor must give up the urge to micro manage the daily events of the church. S/he leads by both authority and power. Must articulate the values and vision for the leadership (¶205)

DEVELOPING HUMAN RESOURCES (cont.)

	BASIC FAMILY (1-50)	EXTENDED FAMILY (51-150)	FAMILY ENTERPRISE (151-350)	CORPORATE ENTERPRISE (350+)
	Pastor not to make decisions for the group. (¶72)	Pastor not to make decisions for the group. (¶116)	Pastor participates in the decision making process as a valued source of information for the guiding coalition. May not make decisions for the group, but the group often makes a decision based on pastor's suggestion or direction. (¶157)	Enacting change requires permission of the pastor. (¶197)
	If the pastor leads, it is by the influence gained by identifying with the patron/matron. Pastor is a figurehead leader hired to help the real leader accomplish what s/he thinks is important. (¶75)	To be successful, the pastor needs to identify with the patron group. More important to be in the stands with the parents at the high school ball games than in the study preparing sermons. Pastor leads by influence gained by identifying with the patron group. (¶118)	Pastor leads by participation and authority shared with the board. S/he must identify with the values and vision of the leadership group.	Pastor is charged with providing vision and direction to the organization. (¶204) Role of the board is to see that the decision the pastor has made gets carried out. (¶197)
	Pastor expected to be a part of the family; expected to work for what family members receive: thanks, a good meal, and a place to sleep. (¶78)	Spreads the cost around a little better; often pays the pastor a better salary. (¶119)	Church is hiring a manager; will attempt to pay what a good manager should be making. (¶159)	Pays what it costs to have the expected level of leadership. (¶206)
	Everybody knows what the pastor is being paid. (¶78)	Everybody knows what the pastor is being paid. (¶119)	Not everybody knows how much the pastor is being paid, but everybody on the board and probably a few key others have this information. (¶159)	Only the finance committee knows how much the pastor is being paid, and in some cases, only a personnel subcommittee of the finance committee. (¶206)

	BASIC FAMILY (1-50)	EXTENDED FAMILY (51-150)	FAMILY ENTERPRISE (151-350)	CORPORATE ENTERPRISE (350+)
BUDGETING	No formal budget; spending is based on the current needs as determined by the patron/matron. (¶ 79)	No formal budget; spending is based on the current needs as determined by the guiding coalition. (¶ 120)	Formal budget. Not based on this year's needs; based last year's spending and funds available. (¶ 160)	Formal budget. In some cases, funded from reserve accounts; available to staff and departments as needed. In other cases, not fully funded and spending is only funded as money becomes available. (¶ 207)
	Pastor has no authority to spend money; must often obtain approval for standard supplies. (¶ 79)	Pastor must get approval to spend money on anything other than stand-ard supplies; has about the same ability to spend money as an office man-ager in an agency owned by someone else. (¶ 121)	Pastor has the authority to see that the normal operational expenses are incurred and paid, but not to initiate new spending. (¶ 160)	Budget process carried out almost entirely by the paid professional staff and approved by the board. (¶ 208)
	High percentage of the total raised comes from the patron/matron, who holds the power of funding. (¶ 81)	High percentage of the total raised comes from the guiding coalition; it holds the power of funding. (¶ 122)	Funding spread out across a broader portion of the membership. (¶ 161) Guiding coalition has the ability to influence the direction of the church by the trust the people put in them; do not have the ability to force issues by threatening to withhold the giving of their own funds. (¶ 162) Their combined giving is usually not 20% of total raised. (¶ 161)	Funding is very broad. The combined giving of the largest donors is often less than 10% of the total raised and they may or may not be considered part of the guiding coalition. (¶ 209)
			Fund raising is both formal and informal. Most of the funding comes from regular individual giving; formal fund raising campaigns also conducted for specific projects. (¶ 163)	Fund raising is both formal and informal. Most of the funding comes from regular individual giving; formal fund raising campaigns also conducted for specific projects. (¶ 210)

	BASIC FAMILY (1-50)	EXTENDED FAMILY (51-150)	FAMILY ENTERPRISE (151-350)	CORPORATE ENTERPRISE (350+)
BUDGETING (cont.)	Treasurer functions as a controller and may be the patron/matron. (¶82)	The treasurer is the controller for the group. His/her decision is final and in many churches s/he can override a decision made by the official church board. (¶120)		
SUPERVISION	Provided by the informal social network. (¶83)	Provided by the informal social network. (¶124)	Provided by the leaders of the particular programs. These leaders, also volunteers, are led and supervised by the pastor or paid staff. (¶165) Pastor is responsible as manager to supervise all of the staff. (¶167)	Supervision of volunteers, is provided by the staff member in charge of the particular program, and by leaders developed within the programs. (¶213) One full time minister may be charged with supervising the rest of the staff. (¶212)
	Informal and undocumented. Informal system values relationships more than tasks or accomplishments. People celebrate with each other over each accomplishment, and support each other through each failure. (¶84)	Most workers are unsupervised most of the time. While anyone can criticize the work of anyone else, the group informally decides whether the criticism is valid and just. People learn their place in the system. (¶125)	Supervision is relationship oriented more often than it is results oriented. The system highly values the goal of personal growth of the individual, and will often put that goal ahead of task goals. (¶166)	Programs have a life of their own and in true bureaucratic style, leaders come and go. It is more likely that a person will be encouraged to drop a particular responsibility than that the program will be changed to fit the person. (¶214)

	BASIC FAMILY (1-50)	EXTENDED FAMILY (51-150)	FAMILY ENTERPRISE (151-350)	CORPORATE ENTERPRISE (350+)
SUPERVISION *(cont.)*	Relationships are more important than results. Relationships form the basis of the desired results. (¶ 55)	Relationships valued more than tasks or accomplishments. Poor performance will be tolerated from a friend, but poor relationships from a high performer will not be tolerated. More concern for people than for production. (¶ 125)	Still a desire to have more concern for people than for production. Conflict arises when that desire is disregarded for the sake of growth or some other success. (¶ 166)	Church would like to value relationships more than results, but results guide the supervision style most of the time. Concern for people shows up in the attempt to help individuals find a place of service that fits their growth needs. (¶ 214)
	No formal performance evaluations.	No formal performance evaluations. Evaluations are entirely subjective; praise or criticism is spontaneous. (¶ 127)	Still a desire to have more concern for people than for production. Conflict arises when that desire is disregarded for the sake of growth or some other success. (¶ 166)	Paid staff have an annual performance evaluation and frequently they will also have a six month progress check up. (¶ 201)
	Pastor may be used by the patron/matron to supervise other members of the family, even in matters not related to the church. (¶ 85)	Pastor must accomplish his or her supervision primarily as a mentor and occasionally as a mediator. The guiding coalition maintains control of most of the management functions, and the structure is not complicated enough to need much in the way of mediation or integration of vertical and horizontal interactions between different levels and units of the organization. Pastor must become part of the operating group if s/he is to guide volunteer growth and development. (¶ 128)	Pastor functions as a mediator and mentor, and also as a manager. (¶ 167)	

	BASIC FAMILY (1-50)	EXTENDED FAMILY (51-150)	FAMILY ENTERPRISE (151-350)	CORPORATE ENTERPRISE (350+)
EVALUATION	Spiritual development of participants is evaluated subjectively, not with measurable criteria, perhaps to control wayward behavior. (¶ 88)	The ongoing formative evaluation is useful and effective in the eyes of the patron group but is often frustrating and upsetting to pastor. (¶ 87)	Outcome of spiritual development of participants evaluated without measurable criteria or structured analysis. (¶ 171)	From time to time participant surveys are conducted to identify interests and satisfaction levels. (¶ 217)

Dr. Charles Crow – charlscrow@outlook.com

About the Author

Michael grew up in South Florida in a troubled home. Having completed the ninth grade, he quit school in 1965 and joined the U.S. Navy. He made two tours to Viet Nam on the U.S.S. Ranger, CVA61, and U.S.S. Enterprise, CVA65. He was honorably discharged as a 2nd class petty officer, jet mechanic in 1969. He earned a GED high school equivalence diploma while in the Navy. Michael married Barbara in the same year he was discharged from the Navy. He worked 2 years at Pratt &

Whitney Aircraft in West Palm Beach. After failing in an attempt to start his own construction business he worked as a carpenter and cabinetmaker. In 1973 he was invited to church by a coworker, and while attending a revival in the West Palm Beach, Florida, First Church of the Nazarene, he became a Believer in the Lord Jesus Christ. It was here that Michael first sensed the call to ministry and served as an Assistant Pastor under Rev. John Sexton for 3 years, from 1976 to 1979. In 1979 he and his wife Barbara, and their two daughters, Laura and Pamela, moved to Colorado Springs, Colorado to attend Nazarene Bible College. Upon graduation in 1982 they accepted a call to a mission church in Covington, Louisiana. They served that congregation from 1982 until 1989. In 1989 Michael changed his affiliation to the Church of God (Anderson) and pastored the First Church of God in Covington. While there, Michael also served as principal of Covington Christian Academy. In 1991, serving as contractor, Michael and the church relocated and constructed a new facility, changing the name to Landmark Church of God. In 1994 Michael accepted a call to pastor Welcome Home Church of God in West Monroe, Louisiana, where he served until 2008. In 2008 he and Barbara moved to Oklahoma City, Oklahoma where Michael attended Southwestern Christian University. In 2009 he graduated Cum Laude with a Bachelor degree in leadership. The following year he started graduate school and graduated with a Master of Ministry degree in 2010. In 2009 he was honored to teach undergraduate classes while attending graduate school. He began teaching the

Bible and ministry classes offered by Mid-America Christian University as an adjunct instructor. In 2015 Michael became a full time faculty member in the College of Adult and Graduate Studies at Mid-America Christian University. In his current capacity he teaches the undergraduate ministry and Bible classes and has written courses in Inductive Bible Study, Romans, Synoptic Gospels, Christian Theology and Christian Ethics.

Made in the USA
San Bernardino, CA
08 August 2018